THE SENSE OF AN ENDING

STUDIES IN THE THEORY OF FICTION

Time cannot exist without a soul
(to count on it).

ARISTOTLE

      a more severe,
More harassing master would extemporize
Subtler, more urgent proof that the theory
Of poetry is the theory of life

As it is, in the intricate evasions of as,
In things seen and unseen, created from nothingness,
The heavens, the hells, the worlds, the longed-for lands.

WALLACE STEVENS

The Sense of an Ending

STUDIES IN THE THEORY OF FICTION
with a New Epilogue

Frank Kermode

OXFORD
UNIVERSITY PRESS
2000

OXFORD

UNIVERSITY PRESS

Oxford New York
Athens Auckland Bangkok Bogotá Buenos Aires Calcutta
Cape Town Chennai Dar es Salaam Delhi Florence Hong Kong
Istanbul Karachi Kuala Lumpur Madrid Melbourne Mexico City
Mumbai Nairobi Paris São Paulo Singapore Taipei Tokyo
Toronto Warsaw
and associated companies in
Berlin Ibadan

Copyright © 1966, 1967, 2000 by Oxford University Press, Inc.

First published by Oxford University Press, New York 1967

First issued as an Oxford University Press paperback, 1968

by Oxford University Press, Inc.,
198 Madison Avenue, New York, New York 10016

Oxford is a registered trademark of Oxford University Press

Library of Congress Cataloging-in-Publication Data
Kermode, Frank, 1919-
The sense of an ending : studies in the theory of fiction : with a
new epilogue / Frank Kermode. -- [New ed.]
p. cm.
Lectures delivered as the Mary Flexner Lectures, Bryn Mawr
College, fall 1965, under the title The long perspectives.
Includes bibliographical references
ISBN 0-19-513612-8
1. Literature--Philosophy. I. Title.
PN45.K44   2000
801--dc21   99-43613

1 3 5 7 9 8 6 4 2

Printed in the United States of America

IN MEMORIAM
J.P.K.
1894–1966

TABLE OF CONTENTS

PREFACE

THIS BOOK consists of the Mary Flexner Lectures given at Bryn Mawr College in the fall of 1965. Having honoured me by the invitation to deliver them, the College increased my debt beyond the possibility of repayment by its hospitality during the six weeks of my stay. To the President, the Faculty, and the students (who contributed so much in discussion) I therefore make this inadequate gesture of gratitude, and I know that none of them will feel slighted if I specially mention the sense of obligation my wife and I feel toward Mary Woodworth.

There are also debts contracted earlier; that I own them but briefly makes them no smaller, nor the sequel better able to satisfy the creditors. Much of the preliminary reading, thinking, and talking was done during an idyllic stay at the Center of Advanced Studies, Wesleyan University. Paul Horgan, the Director, I think, needs no assurance of my affection and gratitude; nor do my friends on the Wesleyan faculty. Two other friends I must mention, because they struggled with and improved early drafts: R.J. Kauffman of Rochester University, and J.B. Trapp of the Warburg Institute.

The purpose of the book being rather to make suggestions, to initiate discussion, than to settle any of the problems it raises, I found myself in some difficulty when I came to pre-

pare it for the press. I had originally intended to write long
notes and appendices, partly to acknowledge more fully the influence of certain books, and refer to many others which had
perhaps affected the course of my thinking, but dropped out of
the argument. Now I see that this would probably diminish
whatever penetrating force these explorations may have, and
that my best policy was rather to keep notes to a minimum,
and conduct any secondary inquiries that I am capable of in
some other place. I have therefore revised the text without
much substantive alteration; the lectures are a little longer than
they were, but stand here much as they were when I delivered
them at Bryn Mawr in October and November 1965. The title
of the series was originally *The Long Perspectives*. I hope that
the change is approved at Bryn Mawr.

Bristol   F.K.
December 1966

THE SENSE OF AN ENDING

I

...then the Last Judgment begins, & its Vision is Seen by the Imaginative Eye of Every one according to the situation he holds.

BLAKE

we can only
Walk in temperate London, our educated city,
Wishing to cry as freely as they did who died
In the Age of Faith. We have our loneliness
And our regret with which to build an eschatology.

PETER PORTER

The End

It is not expected of critics as it is of poets that they should help us to make sense of our lives; they are bound only to attempt the lesser feat of making sense of the ways we try to make sense of our lives. This series of talks is devoted to such an attempt, and I am well aware that neither good books nor good counsel have purged it of ignorance and dull vision; but I take comfort from the conviction that the topic is infallibly interesting, and especially at a moment in history when it may be harder than ever to accept the precedents of sense-making—to believe that any earlier way of satisfying one's need to know the shape of life in relation to the perspectives of time will suffice.

You remember the golden bird in Yeats's poem—it sang of what was past and passing and to come, and so interested a drowsy emperor. In order to do that, the bird had to be 'out of nature'; to speak humanly of becoming and knowing is the task of pure being, and this is humanly represented in the poem by an artificial bird. 'The artifice of eternity' is a striking periphrasis for 'form,' for the shapes which console the dying generations. In this respect it makes little difference—though it makes some—whether you believe the age of the world to be six thousand years or five thousand million years, whether you think time will have a stop or that the world is eternal; there is still a need to speak humanly of a life's importance in relation to it—a need in the moment of existence to belong, to be related to a beginning and to an end.

The physician Alkmeon observed, with Aristotle's approval, that men die because they cannot join the beginning and the end. What they, the dying men, can do is to imagine a significance for themselves in these unremembered but imaginable events. One of the ways in which they do this is to make objects in which everything is that exists in concord with everything else, and nothing else is, implying that this arrangement mirrors the dispositions of a creator, actual or possible:

> . . . as the *Primitive Forms* of all
> (If we compare great things with small)
> Which without *Discord* or *Confusion* lie,
> In that strange *Mirror* of the *Deitie*.

Such models of the world make tolerable one's moment between beginning and end, or at any rate keep us drowsy emperors awake. There are other prophets beside the golden bird, and we are capable of deciding that they are false, or obsolete. I shall be talking not only about the persistence of fictions but about their truth, and also about their decay. There is the question, also, of our growing suspicious of fictions in general. But it seems that we still need them. Our poverty—to borrow that rich concept from Wallace Stevens—is great enough, in a world which is not our own, to necessitate a continuous preoccupation with the changing fiction.

I begin by discussing fictions of the End—about ways in which, under varying existential pressures, we have imagined the ends of the world. This, I take it, will provide clues to the ways in which fictions, whose ends are consonant with origins, and in concord, however unexpected, with their precedents, satisfy our needs. So we begin with Apocalypse, which ends, transforms, and is concordant.

Broadly speaking, apocalyptic thought belongs to rectilinear rather than cyclical views of the world, though this is not a sharp distinction; and even in Jewish thought there was no true apocalyptic until prophecy failed, for Jewish apocalyptic belongs to what scholars call the Intertestamentary Period. But basically one has to think of an ordered series of events which ends, not in a great New Year, but in a final Sabbath. The events derive their significance from a unitary system, not from their correspondence with events in other cycles.

This changes the events themselves, and the temporal relations between them. In Homer, we are told, the Odyssean episodes are related by their correspondence with a cyclic ritual; the time between them is insignificant or null. Virgil, describing the progress of Aeneas from the broken city of Troy to a Rome standing for empire without end, is closer to our traditional apocalyptic, and that is why his *imperium* has been incorporated into Western apocalyptic as a type of the City of God. And in the journey of Aeneas the episodes are related internally; they all exist under the shadow of the end. Erich Auerbach makes a similar point in the opening chapter of *Mimesis*, where he contrasts the story of the scar of Odysseus with the story of the sacrifice of Isaac—the second story has continually to be modified by reference to what is known of the divine

plan from the Creation to the Last Days: it is perpetually
open to history, to reinterpretation—one remembers how
central the story was to Kierkegaard—in terms of changed
human ways of speaking about the single form of the
world. *The Odyssey* is not, in this way, open. Virgil and
Genesis belong to our end-determined fictions; their stories
are placed at what Dante calls the point where all times
are present, *il punto a cui tutti li tempi son presenti;* or
within the shadow of it. It gives each moment its fullness.
And although for us the End has perhaps lost its naïve
imminence, its shadow still lies on the crises of our fictions;
we may speak of it as *immanent.*

This is a position I shall try to justify in my second talk.
Meanwhile let me assume it. In their general character
our fictions have certainly moved away from the simplicity
of the paradigm; they have become more 'open.' But they
still have, and so far as one is capable of prediction must
continue to have, a real relation to simpler fictions about
the world. Apocalypse is a radical instance of such fictions
and a source of others. I shall be speaking of it both as
type and source. In view of my own limitations and because the end of one's lecture is always immanent, I shall
go in for drastic foreshortenings; but if I concentrate on
aspects of the topic important to my argument, I do so,
I hope, without falsifying the others.

The Bible is a familiar model of history. It begins at the
beginning ('In the beginning . . .') and ends with a vision
of the end ('Even so, come, Lord Jesus'); the first book is
Genesis, the last Apocalypse. Ideally, it is a wholly concordant structure, the end is in harmony with the beginning, the middle with beginning and end. The end, Apocalypse, is traditionally held to resume the whole structure,

which it can only do by figures predictive of that part of it which has not been historically revealed. The Book of Revelation made its way only slowly into the canon—it is still unacceptable to Greek Orthodoxy—perhaps because of learned mistrust of over-literal interpretation of the figures. But once established it showed, and continues to show, a vitality and resource that suggest its consonance with our more naïve requirements of fiction.

Men, like poets, rush 'into the middest,' *in medias res,* when they are born; they also die *in mediis rebus,* and to make sense of their span they need fictive concords with origins and ends, such as give meaning to lives and to poems. The End they imagine will reflect their irreducibly intermediary preoccupations. They fear it, and as far as we can see have always done so; the End is a figure for their own deaths. (So, perhaps, are all ends in fiction, even if represented, as they are for example by Kenneth Burke, as cathartic discharges.)

It is sometimes argued—as by those very different critics, D. H. Lawrence and Dr. Austin Farrar—that behind Revelation there lies a strictly inexplicable set of myths that have been overlaid by later topical applications; but what human need can be more profound than to humanize the common death? When we survive, we make little images of moments which have seemed like ends; we thrive on epochs. Fowler observes austerely that if we were always quite serious in speaking of 'the end of an epoch' we should live in ceaseless transition; recently Mr. Harold Rosenberg has been quite seriously saying that we do. Scholars are devoted to the epoch, and philosophers—notably Ortega y Gasset and Jaspers—have tried to give the concept definition. The matter is entirely in our own

hands, of course; but our interest in it reflects our deep
need for intelligible Ends. We project ourselves—a small,
humble elect, perhaps—past the End, so as to see the structure whole, a thing we cannot do from our spot of time
in the middle.

Apocalypse depends on a concord of imaginatively recorded past and imaginatively predicted future, achieved
on behalf of us, who remain 'in the middest.' Its predictions, though figurative, *can* be taken literally, and as the
future moves in on us we may expect it to conform with
the figures. Many difficulties arise from this expectation.
We ask such questions as, who is the Beast from the Land?
the Woman Clothed with the Sun? What is meant by this
number, and to what events do the Seven Seals refer?
Where, on the body of history, shall we look for the scars
of that three-and-a-half years' reign? What is Babylon, who
is the Knight Faithful and True? We may be sure that we
can from our special point of vantage work out the divisions of history in accordance with these figures, and that
we must be right, if only because the state of the world
shows so clearly that the second coming is at hand, *donec
finiatur mundus corruptionis.* The great majority of interpretations of Apocalypse assume that the End is pretty
near. Consequently the historical allegory is always having
to be revised; time discredits it. And this is important.
Apocalypse can be disconfirmed without being discredited.
This is part of its extraordinary resilience. It can also
absorb changing interests, rival apocalypses, such as the
Sibylline writings. It is patient of change and of historiographical sophistications. It allows itself to be diffused,
blended with other varieties of fiction—tragedy, for example, myths of Empire and of Decadence—and yet it can

survive in very naïve forms. Probably the most sophisticated of us is capable at times of naïve reactions to the End.

Let us look for a moment at some features of naïve
apocalyptism. The early Christians were the first to experience the disconfirmation of literal predictions; it has been
said that the apostasies of the second century were the
consequence of this 'eschatological despair,' as Bultmann
calls it. But literal disconfirmation is thwarted by typology,
arithmology, and perhaps by the buoyancy of chiliasts in
general. Thus a mistaken prediction can be attributed to
an error of calculation, either in arithmetic or allegory.
And if you insist that Nero is Antichrist, or Frederick II
the Emperor of the Last Days, you need not be too de-
pressed if your choice should die too early, since at this
level of historical abstraction you can always believe he
will return at a convenient season; and you will even find
Sibylline texts to support you.

Given this freedom, this power to manipulate data in
order to achieve the desired consonance, you can of course
arrange for the End to occur at pretty well any desired
date, but the most famous of all predicted Ends is A.D.
1000. It is now thought that earlier historians exaggerated
the 'Terrors' of that year, but it need not be doubted that
it produced a characteristic apocalypse-crisis. The opinion
of St. Augustine, that the millennium was the first thousand years of the Christian era, supported the feeling that
the world was reaching its term, and that the events of
Apocalypse, already given memorable iconographic form,
were to ensue. The Terrors and Decadence are two of the
recurring elements in the apocalyptic pattern; Decadence
is usually associated with the hope of renovation. Another
permanent feature of the pattern was also illustrated in

the crisis of the year 1000, and this I shall call clerkly scepticism. The Church frowned on precise predictions of the End. One such protest was the *Libellus de Antechristo* of Adso. He was a monk who in 954 argued that the end of the world cannot be predicted, and in any case cannot come until the full restoration of the Empire (ultimately a Sibylline doctrine). It can only happen after a Frankish emperor, following a peaceful universal reign, has deposited his sceptre on the Mount of Olives. The Church persistently tried to de-mythologize Apocalypse, though obviously Adso was discrediting arithmological fictions by substituting what seem to us equally fantastic imperial fictions. In fact the mythology of Empire and of Apocalypse are very closely related. Anyway, there was something that might be called scepticism among the learned—a recognition that arithmetical predictions of the End are bound to be disconfirmed.

When the year 1000 came, there were some portents, and there was a brief but Sibylline *entente* between Emperor and Pope (Otto III and Sylvester II, so much hated by Protestant historians). Seals were issued bearing imperial legends; one had an allegorical figure of Rome and the inscription *renovatio imperii Romani*. The Emperor's coronation robe was embroidered with scenes from Apocalypse. And Henri Focillon, in his book *L'An mil*, can argue that the year actually was significant, marking an epoch, even though it lapsed without universal catastrophe. Naturally there were those who simply thought the calculations were wrong, that we should perhaps count 1000 from the Passion rather than from the Nativity, so that the Day would come in 1033. And this is something that occurs regularly in the literature; the Protestant com-

mentators sometimes counted from the last of the perse-
cutions, sometimes from the conversion of Constantine,
in order to defer that interesting date, the moment of the
loosing of the Beast, to a time when he could be identified
with some intolerable papal presumption or with some
particularly vicious pope. More sophisticated calculations,
based on the Seven Seals, or the period spent by the
Woman Clothed with the Sun in the wilderness, could
produce other dates as near one's own moment as desirable.

Focillon's treatment of the year 1000 reflects his interest
in the way not only the millennium but the century and
other fundamentally arbitrary chronological divisions—we
might simply call them *saecula*—are made to bear the
weight of our anxieties and hopes; they are, as he remarks,
'intemporal,' but we project them onto history, making it
'a perpetual calendar of human anxiety.' They help us
to find ends and beginnings. They explain our senescence,
our renovations; when we associate them with empire we
are celebrating our desire for human kinds of order; when
we find rational objections to them we indulge our powers
of rational censorship in such matters; and when we refuse
to be dejected by disconfirmed predictions we are only
asserting a permanent need to live by the pattern rather
than the fact, as indeed we must.

There are famous *saecula*, Ends of which everyone is
aware, and in which we may take a complex comfort, as
in the nineteenth-century *fin de siècle*, where all the elements of the apocalyptic paradigm clearly co-exist. But
there are many others less famous, to show how radical
an element in our thinking about the world's design this
brooding on apocalypse must be. The Bible and the Sybil-
line oracles, mingled with Neo-Platonic speculation and

with any other mysterious data available, will provide any date for the End, and the necessary supporting evidence is always available. A.D. 195 was a Sibylline conjecture; 948, 1000, 1033, 1236, 1260, 1367, 1420, 1588, 1666 are other guesses. We must count Dante and perhaps Shakespeare among the major poets interested in the signs of historical apocalypse, and among the mathematicians, Napier and Newton. And as Focillon observed, the world sometimes seems to collaborate with our apocalypse; students of the English sixteenth century will recall that the *novae*, especially the one in Cassiopeia in 1572, and the solar eclipse of the late years of the century, seemed to confirm that upon men who thought themselves to be living 'in the dregs of time' there had come 'the signs of the approaching of the Lord to judgment.' They will also remember the sceptics of the period, and reflect that after so much talk of senescence there was soon to be a great outburst of renovatory chiliasm. And perhaps they will also reflect upon the interesting revival of imperial mythologies at both the French and the English courts of the period.

There is an instance of the way in which apparently unrelated *fin-de-siècle* myths grow together. But there is one important element in this apocalyptic pattern which I have as yet hardly mentioned. This is the myth, if we can call it that, of Transition. Before the End there is a period which does not properly belong either to the End or to the *saeculum* preceding it. It has its own characteristics. This period of Transition seems not to have been defined until the end of the twelfth century; but the definition then arrived at—by Joachim of Flora—has proved to be remarkably enduring. Its origin is in the three-and-a-half-year reign of the Beast which, in Revelation, precedes the

Last Days. Joachim, who died in 1202, divided history
into three phases, a division based on the Trinity; the
last transition would begin in 1260, a date arrived at by
multiplying forty-two by thirty, the number of years in
each generation between Abraham and Christ. This was
accordingly taken to be the date of the coming of Antichrist, and consequently of the figure called the Knight
Faithful and True, *fidelis et verax*, identified with the
last emperor. These prophecies had a long life; not only
Dante, at the end of the century, but Hegel and others
much later, took them seriously. In the mid-thirteenth
century the prophecies were of the utmost urgency. Frederick II was cast as Beast, or as *fidelis et verax*, depending
on whether you adhered to one party or the other. The
Benedictines argued that the figure who corresponded,
for the third age, to Adam in the first and Abraham in the
second, was Saint Benedict. The Spiritual Franciscans
said it was St. Francis. The Emperor was important to all
interpretations; this was the age of the *Dies Irae*, in which
the Sibyl is coupled with David as an authoritative witness
to the Last Days.

The death of Frederick ten years early, in 1250, could
not halt Joachite speculation. It was condemned in 1260,
and subsequently thrived best in unorthodox contexts.
Its *evangelium aeternum* was transmitted by the Brethren
of the Free Spirit, by the Anabaptists and by Boehme, by
the Family of Love and the Ranters. The Jesus of Blake's
Everlasting Gospel is the Christ of Joachim's third phase.
Some aspects of this brand of apocalypse survive in D. H.
Lawrence. More dangerously, the ideology of National
Socialism incorporated Joachite elements; "the Third
Reich" is itself a Joachite expression. And the notion of an

End-dominated age of transition has passed into our consciousness, and modified our attitudes to historical pattern.
As Ruth Kestenberg-Gladstein observes, 'the Joachite triad
made it inevitable that the present become "a mere transitional stage," and leaves people with a sense of living at
a turning-point of time.'

Thus apocalypse, which resumes the Bible, projects its
neat, naïve patterns on to history. Simplifying, and leaving
out much I was tempted to gossip about, I will now say
a word about apocalyptic doctrines of crisis, decadence,
and empire, and of the division of history into mutually
significant phases and transitions; with a word on disconfirmation, the inevitable fate of detailed eschatological
predictions.

The imperial aspect is greatly illuminated by Norman
Cohn's book, *The Pursuit of the Millennium,* with its account of the popular survival of Sibylline emperor cults.
The tradition of those passionate artisan prophets, who
assumed the role of the Emperor of the Last Days and led
their free-spirited followers in search of the new Jerusalem,
was still alive in the nineteenth century, as a sort of pro-
letarian parallel to the more sophisticated imperialism of
the ruling classes in Germany and England. Eric Hobsbawm's book, *Primitive Rebels,* studies several such movements. Lazzaretti, for example, prophesied the coming of
a monarch who would reconcile church and people; later
he proclaimed himself the Messiah, preaching a modified
Joachism, which said that there had been Kingdoms of
Grace and of Justice, and that we were in the transition
between the second and the third Kingdom, that of the
Holy Ghost. He nominated 1878 for the crisis; and in that
year died both Vittorio Emmanuele I and Pius IX. Lazza-

retti moved to succeed them both, and was killed in the attempt. Thus a popular uprising of only ninety years back
repeats the pattern discernible in the relations between
Pope and Emperor in the year 1000, a relation both Sibylline and Joachite. Hobsbawm can even add that the attempt on Togliatti in 1948 was taken by some Italian
Communists as a signal that the Day had come; they were
surviving members of the Lazzaretti movement, still,
against all expectation, persisting underground, presumably with the date recalculated.

The study of apocalypse can be a heady one. For in-
stance, there appeared in 1963 a book by Fr. Cyril Marystone entitled *The Coming Type of the End of the World.*
This work is dedicated to the Woman Clothed with the
Sun, 'the Mother of Christ and the Church—who is perse-
cuted by the Great Red Dragon.' The author divides fu-
ture history into three periods, the present 'modern anti-
Christian,' the 'Period of the Universal Victory of the
Christian Church on Earth,' and the 'Period of the Great
Apostasy.' Published in 1963, the book predicts atomic
war and world victory for Communism in 1964. The Great
Monarch will come in 1966, and in consort with the Great
Pope will achieve world victory, the reform of the Church,
the conversion of the separated, and a universal Holy
Roman Empire. Later on there is to be a Great Apostasy,
and Antichrist will reign for three and a half years, where-
upon the Last Days supervene.

In a world not short of crazy sects, and perhaps in no
need of spurious apocalypses, such a work may seem un-
worthy of your attention. But it will bear thinking about,
if only as a full statement of this potent imperial myth. It
is a well-written book, with an exceptionally valuable sur-

vey of earlier apocalyptic prophecy; and one could well take it to be an expression, in traditional figures, of a widely shared sense of crisis. Shakespeare and Spenser would have understood its language. Father Marystone is quite capable of a rational compromise between his predictions and those of doctrinaire Marxism, and he is familiar with the more sophisticated modern apocalyptism of such as Berdyaev. But he works the vein of naïve apocalypse. His list of former prophecies includes those of Hrabanus Maurus and Adso, who held that the last Emperor must be a Frankish king. Instead of saying they were wrong, he argues that this figure must be the present heir to the French throne; and with the utmost urgency (since the time is so short) he joins in the old argument as to who this might be. The book—half of which is in the form of appendices added in haste, because there was no time to rewrite it when fresh material came up—the book is a paradigm of crisis, of a way of thinking about the present as being what theologians call totally end-directed. We may be sure that the failure of 1964, or even, so far, of 1965, to produce atomic war and the burning of Paris will not have dismayed the author; his book is founded on centuries of disconfirmed apocalyptic prediction.

This indifference to disconfirmation was the subject of some interesting research, a few years ago, by the American sociologist Festinger. He found a thriving sect and infiltrated some of his research students into it. This group believed that the end was at hand, and that they would be flown off in flying saucers just before the cataclysm. The students attended all meetings, and retired nightly to hotel bedrooms to write up their reports. They were present at the final countdown, on the Day, and were able to observe that for most of the members of the sect disconfirmation was quickly followed by the invention of new end-fictions and new calculations. Festinger had previously noted that such sects characteristically sought to restore the pattern of prophecy rather than to abandon it, and on this erects a general doctrine, very interesting in the present connection, of what he calls *consonance*.

In fact this desire for consonance in the apocalyptic data, and our tendency to be derisive about it, seem to me equally interesting. Each manifests itself, in the presence of the other, in most of our minds. We are all ready to be sceptical about Father Marystone, but we are most of us given to some form of 'centurial mysticism,' and even to more extravagant apocalyptic practices: a point I shall be taking up in my fourth talk. What it seems to come to is this. Men in the middest make considerable imaginative investments in coherent patterns which, by the provision of an end, make possible a satisfying consonance with the origins and with the middle. That is why the image of the end can never be *permanently* falsified. But they also, when awake and sane, feel the need to show a marked respect for things as they are; so that there is a recurring need for adjustments in the interest of reality as well as of control.

This has relevance to literary plots, images of the grand temporal consonance; and we may notice that there is the same co-existence of naïve acceptance and scepticism here as there is in apocalyptic. Broadly speaking, it is the popular story that sticks most closely to established conventions; novels the clerisy calls 'major' tend to vary them, and to vary them more and more as time goes by. I shall be talk-

ing about this in some detail later, but a few brief illus-
trations might be useful now. I shall refer chiefly to one
aspect of the matter, the falsification of one's expectation
of the end.

The story that proceeded very simply to its obviously
predestined end would be nearer myth than novel or
drama. Peripeteia, which has been called the equivalent,
in narrative, of irony in rhetoric, is present in every story
of the least structural sophistication. Now peripeteia depends on our confidence of the end; it is a disconfirmation
followed by a consonance; the interest of having our expectations falsified is obviously related to our wish to reach
the discovery or recognition by an unexpected and instructive route. It has nothing whatever to do with any reluc-
tance on our part to get there at all. So that in assimilating
the peripeteia we are enacting that readjustment of expectations in regard to an end which is so notable a feature
of naïve apocalyptic.

And we are doing rather more than that; we are, to look
at the matter in another way, re-enacting the familiar
dialogue between credulity and scepticism. The more dar-
ing the peripeteia, the more we may feel that the work
respects our sense of reality; and the more certainly we
shall feel that the fiction under consideration is one of
those which, by upsetting the ordinary balance of our
naïve expectations, is finding something out for us, something *real*. The falsification of an expectation can be terrible, as in the death of Cordelia; it is a way of finding
something out that we should, on our more conventional
way to the end, have closed our eyes to. Obviously it could
not work if there were not a certain rigidity in the set of
our expectations.

The degree of rigidity is a matter of profound interest in the study of literary fictions. As an extreme case you will find some novel, probably contemporary with yourself, in which the departure from a basic paradigm, the peripeteia in the sense I am now giving it, seems to begin with the first sentence. The schematic expectations of the reader are discouraged immediately. Since by definition one seeks the maximum peripeteia (in this extended sense) in the fiction of one's own time, the best instance I can give is from Alain Robbe-Grillet. He refuses to speak of his 'theory' of the novel; it is the old ones who talk about the need for plot, character, and so forth, who have the theories. And without them one can achieve a new realism, and a narrative in which 'le temps se trouve coupé de la temporalité. Il ne coule plus.' And so we have a novel in which the reader will find none of the gratification to be had from sham temporality, sham causality, falsely certain description, clear story. The new novel 'repeats itself, bisects itself, modifies itself, contradicts itself, without even accumulating enough bulk to constitute a past—and thus a "story," in the traditional sense of the word.' The reader is not offered easy satisfactions, but a challenge to creative co-operation.

When Robbe-Grillet wrote *Les Gommes* he was undoubtedly refining upon certain sophisticated conventions developed by Simenon in the Maigret novels; but in those the dark side of the plot is eventually given a reasonable explanation, whereas in Robbe-Grillet the need for this has gone. Rival versions of the same set of facts can co-exist without final reconciliation. The events of the day are the events of the novel, and on the first page we are told that they will 'encroach upon the ideal order, cunningly introducing an occasional inversion, a discrepancy, a warp, in order to accomplish their work.' The time of the novel is not related to any exterior norm of time. So, in *La Jalousie,* the narrator is explicitly 'unconcerned with chronology,' perceiving only that here and now in which memory, fantasy, anticipation of the future may intrude, though without sharp differentiation. The story does move forward, but without reference to 'real' time, or to the paradigms of real time familiar from conventional novels.

It is a question how far these books could make their effect if we were genuinely, as Robbe-Grillet thinks we should be, indifferent to all conventional expectations. In some sense they must be there to be defeated. Thus, in another novel, *In the Labyrinth,* the soldier who is the central figure only slowly emerges (in so far as he does emerge) from other things, the objects described with equal objectivity, such as the mysterious packet he carries (why is it mysterious? that is a conventional expectation, to be defeated later) or a street, or wallpaper. The soldier has a mission; as you expect to hear about it you are given minute descriptions—of snow on windowsills, of polish on a boot, of the blurred rings left by glasses on a wooden tabletop. There is an unhelpful child, who comes in again and again, confusing one about one's way, asking questions. There is a woman who gives the soldier food, and a photograph mysteriously (why?) related to the soldier himself and what he is doing. It seems he has arrived at the unknown place he seeks; but no, he has not, for he is back at an earlier point in the story, though he does not seem to have been dreaming. He even sees himself in the street. The book makes its own unexpected, unexpectable designs; this is *écriture labyrinthine,* as *Les Gommes* is writing with an eraser. The story ends where it began, within the immediate perceptual field of a narrator. It is always *not* doing things which we unreasonably assume novels ought to do: connect, diversify, explain, make concords, facilitate extrapolations. Certainly there is no temporality, no successiveness. In Robbe-Grillet's latest novel the same character is murdered four times over (an extension of the device already used in *Les Gommes*). This is certainly a shrewd blow at paradigmatic expectations. Still, this is very modern and therefore very extreme. As a method Robbe-Grillet's owes a good deal to those of Sartre and Camus, and it is obvious that both *La Nausée* and *L'Etranger* are strikingly original and unconventional fictions; yet in the view of the younger man, Camus was incapable of breaking completely with the old myths of narrative, the old anthropomorphism, and Robbe-Grillet calls him a tragic humanist. Sartre in his own way is just as old-fashioned, his world 'entièrement tragifié.' And it is true that even in these novels, and much more in *Les Chemins de la liberté* and in *La Peste,* Sartre and Camus are less contemptuous than Robbe-Grillet of paradigm and expectation.

For example, the first chapter of *La Peste* is not so different from one of Scott's leisurely overtures; it talks about the 'setting,' Oran, and although it contains what might be called typological ironies—indications of the ways in which Oran, in the book, might stand for any community, or for some particular communities (France, for example, on the eve of the Occupation)— these are not obtrusive. The 'real' opening follows, and striking though it may be —'When leaving his surgery on the morning of 16 April, Dr. Bernard Rieux felt something soft under his foot'—

it is no great departure from the famous norm of an opening sentence, 'The Marquise went out at five o'clock.' So
at the end: the end of the plague might seem a natural
close, but it goes on, and Rieux, now known to be the
narrator, adds a few words to moralize the situation: in
happy cities which do not like death it is easy to ignore
the existence of the plague bacillus, and so on. This is,
however, not the old ending that panders to temporal
expectations, the sort described (in its comic mode) by
Henry James as 'a distribution at the last of prizes, pen-
sions, husbands, wives, babies, millions, appended para-
graphs, and cheerful remarks.' In fact Camus has put the
conventional opening and close to original use; for without the opening and the close it would certainly be less
easy to argue, as is commonplace, that the book is 'really
about' the Occupation, or 'really about' more abstract issues. The peripeteia is there all right, but it bears more
directly upon the conventions which make it possible. *La
Peste* is what the analysts call 'over-determined,' is suscep-
tible to multiple readings, because of the slightly extra-
paradigmatic way of proceeding I have tried to sketch in.
There is other evidence; it even contains the opening of
a rival novel, intensely conventional, and the sermons are
also peripeteias. *La Peste* is much more like a 'novel' than
Dans le labyrinthe, but it has anti-novelistic devices; as all
good novels, on the French definition of the anti-novel,
must have.

    Let me, to get the situation clearer, choose at random
one more novel, an older one again, which has the advantage of being universally regarded as a remarkable master-
piece: Dostoevsky's *The Idiot.* To put it at its lowest, this
novel abounds in surprising things. But it starts off with

the Warsaw train rapidly approaching St. Petersburg 'at about nine o'clock in the morning at the end of November,' and tells us that the train contains Prince Myshkin and Rogozhin. They are elaborately described, and the other principal, Nastasya Filippovna, is discussed in some detail before the train gets in. Even Lebedev is there. The prince is called a 'holy fool.' It seems that nothing in the story is being held back. And indeed the book ends, thirteen or fourteen reading hours later, with Rogozhin and Myshkin together beside the dead Nastasya, the corpse with its one hovering fly, the murderer, and the idiot consoling him. Or so it would end, were it not that Dostoevsky found the paradigms convenient in their place; he writes a 'conclusion,' completely perfunctory and traditional, in which he tells you what became of the surviving characters, one of those ends so despised by Henry James.

It would be of little use at this point to introduce more examples. In the *nouveau roman* of Robbe-Grillet there is an attempt at a more or less Copernican change in the relation between the paradigm and the text. In Camus the counter-pointing is less doctrinaire; in Dostoevsky there is no evidence of any theoretical stand at all, simply rich originality within or without, as it chances, normal expectations.

All these are novels which most of us would agree (and it is by a consensus of this kind only that these matters, quite rightly, are determined) to be at least very good. They represent in varying degrees that falsification of simple expectations as to the structure of a future which constitutes peripeteia. We cannot, of course, be denied an end; it is one of the great charms of books that they have to end. But unless we are extremely naïve, as some apoca-

lyptic sects still are, we do not ask that they progress towards that end precisely as we have been given to believe.
In fact we should expect only the most trivial work to conform to pre-existent types.

It is essential to the drift of all these talks that what I
call the scepticism of the clerisy operates in the person of
the reader as a demand for constantly changing, constantly
more subtle, relationships between a fiction and the paradigms, and that this expectation enables a writer much
inventive scope as he works to meet and transcend it. The
presence of such paradigms in fictions may be necessary—
that is a point I shall be discussing later—but if the fictions
satisfy the clerisy, the paradigms will be to a varying but
always great extent attenuated or obscured. The pressure
of reality on us is always varying, as Stevens might have
said: the fictions must change, or if they are fixed, the
interpretations must change. Since we continue to 'prescribe laws to nature'—Kant's phrase, and we do—we shall
continue to have a relation with the paradigms, but we
shall change them to make them go on working. If we
cannot break free of them, we must make sense of them.

If this is true of literary ends, it is also true of theological
responses to apocalypse. For if I am right in my argument,
the sceptical modification of a paradigmatic fiction ought
to be visible in the apocalyptic of the theologians as well
as in other spheres. There has always been some caution
about taking Revelation too simply, and an early insistence
that the End was not subject to human prediction. The
earliest Christians had a sharp experience of disconfirmation, and the text of St. Mark, the least favoured of the
gospels in early days, became important: 'of that day or

that hour no one knows, not even the angels in heaven,
nor the Son, but only the Father.' They had, as Bultmann
puts it, abolished history in favour of eschatology; but it
was a premature abolition. Already in St. Paul and St.
John there is a tendency to conceive of the End as happening at every moment; this is the moment when the
modern concept of *crisis* was born—St. John puns on the
Greek word, which means both 'judgment' and 'separation.' Increasingly the present as 'time-between' came to
mean not the time between one's moment and the *parousia*, but between one's moment and one's death. This
throws the weight of 'End-feeling' on to the moment, the
crisis, but also on to the sacraments. 'In the sacramental
church,' says Bultmann, 'eschatology is not abandoned but
is neutralized in so far as the powers of the beyond are
already working in the present.' No longer imminent, the
End is immanent. So that it is not merely the remnant of
time that has eschatological import; the whole of history,
and the progress of the individual life, have it also, as a
benefaction from the End, now immanent. History and
eschatology, as Collingwood observed, are then the same
thing. Butterfield calls 'every instant... eschatological';
Bultmann says that 'in every moment slumbers the possibility of being the eschatological moment. You must
awake it.'

Variants of this position are common in modern eschatology. It is true that they have early precedents. St. Augustine speaks of the terrors of the End as a figure for
personal death, as Winklhofer calls each death a recurring
parousia. But apocalypse, which included and superseded
prophecy, was itself to be included in tragedy; and tragedy
lost its height and stateliness when the single unritualized

death became the sole point of reference. Literary and theological apocalypse have alike chosen to concentrate upon what was only an implication of the original apocalyptic pattern; this is the way they have responded to modern reality. Of course it should not be said that all modern theologians have departed so far from the archetype. Lawrence jeered at Archdeacon Charles for calling the Kaiser Antichrist, but Josef Pieper, in our own day, is less likely to be scorned for saying that many have been called Antichrist because many have indeed been Antichrist, or types of him, so that Nazism is a 'milder preliminary form of the state of Antichrist,' and so is any other tyranny. And even here we can see that the older, sharply predictive apocalypse, with its precise identifications, has been blurred; eschatology is stretched over the whole of history, the End is present at every moment, the types always relevant.

Karl Popper, in a biting phrase, once called historicism the 'substitution of historical prophecy for conscience.' But of modern eschatology one can say that it has done exactly the opposite, and substituted conscience, or something subtler, for historical prophecy. We shall later notice analogies in modern literary fiction. Meanwhile we can say, I hope, that in talking about our theological analogue we have reached the position of Jaspers, who remarked that to live is to live in crisis; in a world which may or may not have a temporal end, people see themselves much as St. Paul saw the early Christians, men 'upon whom the ends of the ages are come'; and these ends bear down upon every important moment experienced by men in the middest. We can see how what I called naïve apocalyptism has been modified to produce (under the pressure

and relevance of great new systems of knowledge, technological and social change, of human decision itself) a sense
of ends only loosely related to the older predictive apocalypse, and to its simpler notions of decadence, empire,
transition, heavens on earth. Granted that the End becomes a predicament of the individual, we may look back
at these historical patterns with envy, but without any
sense that they can ever again be useful except as fictions
patiently explained.

Death and election are individual matters and became
so early enough in the story. The disconfirmation of the
primary eschatological predictions threw the emphasis on
personal death as well as on to the sacraments; it has been
said that Christianity of all the great religions is the most
anxious, is the one which has laid the most emphasis on
the terror of death. Reformation theology strengthened
this emphasis. In the very period when epic poets were
reviving the Sibylline eschatology for imperial purposes,
the End grew harder and harder to think of as an imminent historical event, and so incidentally did the beginning; so that the duration and structure of time less and
less supported the figures of apocalpse which blossomed
in the glass and the illuminations of the Middle Ages. This
was the moment when the terrors of apocalypse were ab-
sorbed by tragedy. The Renaissance equivalent of the
long Beatus tradition—in sculpture, manuscript, sermon,
and church painting—is *King Lear*. And the process of
sophisticating the paradigm continues. Tragedy, we are
told, must yield to Absurdity; existential tragedy is an
impossibility and *King Lear* is a terrible farce. It would
be interesting to see what a modern painter—Francis Bacon, perhaps—might make of the Beatus types; they might

have terror enough, but the paradigms would be, one feels, deeply submerged.

In the nature of the case this must be so. Yet these old paradigms continue in some way to affect the way we make sense of the world. The notion of crisis, for instance; we are all too familiar with it, and too familiar with the difficulties attending any discussion of it; yet there is a myth of crisis, a very deep and complex one, which we should make more sense of if we could reduce it from the status of myth to the status of fiction. Later on I shall try to do this, and talk about what Focillon calls 'centurial mysticism' and some other elements in crisis-myth—the co-existence and flourishing of many apparently disparate apocalypse-themes like decadence and empire at historical moments otherwise apparently unrelated, though for one reason or another thought 'critical.' The Joachite 'transition' is the historical ancestor of modern crisis; in so far as we claim to live now in a period of perpetual transition we have merely elevated the interstitial period into an 'age' or *saeculum* in its own right, and the age of perpetual transition in technological and artistic matters is understandably an age of perpetual crisis in morals and politics. And so, changed by our special pressures, subdued by our scepticism, the paradigms of apocalypse continue to lie under our ways of making sense of the world.

I have used the theologians and their treatment of apocalypse as a model of what we might expect to find not only in more literary treatments of the same radical fiction, but in the literary treatment of radical fictions in general. The assumptions I have made in doing so I shall try to examine next time. Meanwhile it may be useful to have some kind of summary account of what I've been saying. The main object is the critical business of making sense of some of the radical ways of making sense of the world. Apocalypse and the related themes are strikingly long-lived; and that is the first thing to say tbout them, although the second is that they change. The Johannine acquires the characteristics of the Sibylline Apocalypse, and develops other subsidiary fictions which, in the course of time, change the laws we prescribe to nature, and specifically to time. Men of all kinds act, as well as reflect, as if this apparently random collocation of opinion and predictions were true. When it appears that it cannot be so, they act as if it were true in a different sense. Had it been otherwise, Virgil could not have been *altissimo poeta* in a Christian tradition; the Knight Faithful and True could not have appeared in the opening stanzas of *The Faerie Queene*. And what is far more puzzling, the City of Apocalypse could not have appeared as a modern Babylon, together with the 'shipmen and merchants who were made rich by her' and by the 'inexplicable splendour' of her 'fine linen, and purple and scarlet,' in *The Waste Land*, where we see all these things, as in Revelation, 'come to nought.' Nor is this a matter of literary allusion merely. The Emperor of the Last Days turns up as a Flemish or an Italian peasant, as Queen Elizabeth or as Hitler; the Joachite transition as a Brazilian revolution, or as the Tudor settlement, or as the Third Reich. The apocalyptic types—empire, decadence and renovation, progress and catastrophe—are fed by history and underlie our ways of making sense of the world from where we stand, in the middest.

But the more learned the cleric, whether theologian, poet, or novelist, the 'higher' the kind he practises, the

more subtly are these types overlaid. That which seemed
a straightforward prediction becomes an obscure figure.
As the predictions go wrong, it emerges that it is not merely
upon the people of a certain moment but upon all men
that the ends of the world have come. Apocalypse, which
succeeded prophecy, merges with tragedy; the humble
elect survive not all the kings of the earth as in Revelation,
but the one king whose typical story is enacted before
them. When tragedy established itself in England it did
so in terms of plots and spectacle that had much more to
do with medieval apocalypse than with the *mythos* and
opsis of Aristotle. Later, tragedy itself succumbs to the
pressure of 'demythologizing'; the End itself, in modern
literary plotting loses its downbeat, tonic-and-dominant
finality, and we think of it, as the theologians think of
Apocalypse, as immanent rather than imminent. Thus,
as we shall see, we think in terms of crisis rather than
temporal ends; and make much of subtle disconfirmation
and elaborate peripeteia. And we concern ourselves with
the conflict between the deterministic pattern any plot
suggests, and the freedom of persons within that plot to
choose and so to alter the structure, the relations of beginning, middle, and end.

Naïvely predictive apocalypses implied a strict concordance between beginning, middle, and end. Thus the opening of the seals had to correspond to recorded historical
events. Such a concordance remains a deeply desired object, but it is hard to achieve when the beginning is lost
in the dark backward and abysm of time, and the end is
known to be unpredictable. This changes our views of the
patterns of time, and in so far as our plots honour the
increased complexity of these ways of making sense, it

complicates them also. If we ask for comfort from our
plots it will be a more difficult comfort than that which
the archangel offered Adam:

> How soon hath thy prediction, Seer blest,
> Measur'd this transient World, the race of Time,
> Till time stands fix'd.

But it will be a related comfort. In our world the material
for an eschatology is more elusive, harder to handle. It
may not be true, as the modern poet argues, that we must
build it out of 'our loneliness and regret'; the past has
left us stronger materials than these for our artifice of
eternity. But the artifice of eternity exists only for the
dying generations; and since they choose, alter the shape
of time, and die, the eternal artifice must change. The
golden bird will not always sing the same song, though a
primeval pattern underlies its notes.

In my next talk I shall be trying to explain some of the
ways in which that song changes, and talking about the
relationship between apocalypse and the changing fictions
of men born and dead in the middest. It is a large subject,
because the instrument of change is the human imagination. It changes not only the consoling plot, but the structure of time and the world. One of the most striking things
about it was said by Stevens in one of his adages; and it is
with this suggestive saying that I shall mark the transition
from the first to the second part of my own pattern. 'The
imagination,' said this student of changing fictions, 'the
imagination is always at the end of an era.' Next time we
shall try to see what this means in relation to our problem
of making sense of the ways we make sense of the world.

II

What can be thought must certainly be a fiction.

NIETZSCHE

... the nicer knowledge of
Belief, that what it believes in is not true.

WALLACE STEVENS

Who can deny that things to come are not yet?
Yet already there is in the mind an expectation
of things to come.

ST. AUGUSTINE

C'est par l'effort et le désir que nous avons fait connaissance avec
le temps; nous guidons l'habitude d'estimer le temps selon désirs,
nos efforts, notre volonté propre.

GUYAU, *Le Genèse de l'idée de temps.*

Fictions

ONE of my tasks in this second talk is to answer some of
the questions which I begged in the first. I wanted to
concentrate on eschatological fictions, fictions of the End,
in relation to apocalypse itself; and though I did say something about these as analogous to literary fictions, by means
of which we impose other patterns on historical time, I
did little to justify the analogy. And when I spoke of the
degree to which fictions vary from the paradigmatic base,
I again confined myself largely to straight apocalypse—the
way the type figures were modified, made to refer not to
a common End but to personal death or to crisis, or to
epoch. I mentioned that literary fictions changed in the
same way—perpetually recurring crises of the person, and
the death of that person, took over from myths which
purport to relate one's experience to grand beginnings
and ends. And I suggested that there have been great
changes, especially in recent times when our attitudes to
fiction in general have grown so sophisticated; although
it seems, at the same time, that in 'making sense' of the
world we still feel a need, harder than ever to satisfy because of an accumulated scepticism, to experience that
concordance of beginning, middle, and end which is the

essence of our explanatory fictions, and especially when
they belong to cultural traditions which treat historical
time as primarily rectilinear rather than cyclic.

Obviously I now need to say more about the way I have
been using such words as 'fiction' and 'concordance.' First,
then, let us reflect that it is pretty surprising, given the
range and minuteness of modern literary theory, that nobody, so far as I know, has ever tried to relate the theory
of literary fictions to the theory of fictions in general,
though I think something of the sort may have been in
Ogden's mind when he assembled *Bentham's Theory of
Fictions;* and there are relevant implications, not developed in this direction, in Richards on 'speculative instru-
ments' and what he calls 'experimental submission.' Richards is certainly concerned with the nature and quality of
one's assent to fictions as a means to personal freedom or
perhaps simply to personal comfort.

But that there *is* a simple relation between literary and
other fictions seems, if one attends to it, more obvious than
has appeared. If we think first of modern fictions, it can
hardly be an accident that ever since Nietzsche generalized
and developed the Kantian insights, literature has increasingly asserted its right to an arbitrary and private choice
of fictional norms, just as historiography has become a
discipline more devious and dubious because of our recognition that its methods depend to an unsuspected degree
on myths and fictions. After Nietzsche it was possible to
say, as Stevens did, that 'the final belief must be in a fiction.' This poet, to whom the whole question was of perpetual interest, saw that to think in this way was to post-
pone the End—when the fiction might be said to coincide
with reality—for ever; to make of it a fiction, an imaginary

moment when 'at last' the world of fact and the *mundo* of fiction shall be one. Such a fiction—the last section of *Notes toward a Supreme Fiction* is, appropriately, the place where Stevens gives it his fullest attention—such a fiction of the end is like infinity plus one and imaginary numbers in mathematics, something we know does not exist, but which helps us to make sense of and to move in the world. *Mundo* is itself such a fiction. I think Stevens, who certainly thought we have to make our sense out of whatever materials we find to hand, borrowed it from Ortega. His general doctrine of fictions he took from Vaihinger, from Nietzsche, perhaps also from American pragmatism.

First, an ethical problem. If literary fictions *are* related to all others, then it must be said that they have some dangerous relations. 'The falseness of an opinion is not ... any objection to it,' says Nietzsche, adding that the only relevant question is 'how far the opinion is life-furthering, life-preserving, species-preserving.' A man who thinks this is in some danger of resembling the Cretan Liar, for his opinion can be no less fictive than the opinions to which it alludes. He may be in worse danger; he may be encouraging people who hold the fictive view that death on a large scale is life-furthering and species-preserving. On the one hand you have a relatively innocent theory, a way of coming to terms with the modern way of recognizing the gulf between being and knowing, the sense that nature can always be made to answer our questions, comply with our fictions. This is what Wordsworth curiously and touchingly predicted when he asserted that 'Nature never did betray / The heart that loved her.' In its purely operational form this is the basis of the theoretical physicist's life, since he assumes that there will always be

experimental confirmation for positions arrived at by pure
mathematics. Naturally, the answers, like the questions,
are purely human. 'Nature is patient of interpretation in
terms of laws that happen to interest us,' as Whitehead
remarked. But on the other hand you have the gas-chambers. Alfred Rosenberg used the innocent speculations of
William James, John Dewey, and F. C. S. Schiller to argue
that knowledge was at the service of 'organic' truth, which
he identified with the furthering of the life of what he
called the 'German race.' If the value of an opinion is to
be tested only by its success in the world, the propositions
of dementia can become as valuable as any other fictions.
The validity of one's opinion of the Jews can be proved
by killing six million Jews.

  Hannah Arendt, who has written with clarity and passion on this issue, argues that the philosophical or anti-
philosophical assumptions of the Nazis were not generi-
cally different from those of the scientist, or indeed of any
of us in an age 'where man, wherever he goes, encounters
only himself.' How, in such a situation, can our paradigms
of concord, our beginnings and ends, our humanly ordered
picture of the world satisfy us, make sense? How can apocalypse or tragedy make sense, or more sense than any arbitrary nonsense can be made to make sense? If King Lear
is an image of the promised end, so is Buchenwald; and
both stand under the accusation of being horrible, rootless
fantasies, the one no more true or more false than the
other, so that the best you say is that King Lear does less
harm.

  I think we have to admit that the consciously false apocalypse of the Third Reich and the consciously false apocalypse of King Lear imply equally a recognition that it is

ourselves we are encountering whenever we invent fictions.
There may even be a real relation between certain kinds
of effectiveness in literature and totalitarianism in politics.
But although the fictions are alike ways of finding out
about the human world, anti-Semitism is a fiction of
escape which tells you nothing about death but projects
it onto others; whereas *King Lear* is a fiction that inescapably involves an encounter with oneself, and the image
of one's end. This is one difference; and there is another.
We have to distinguish between myths and fictions. Fictions can degenerate into myths whenever they are not
consciously held to be fictive. In this sense anti-Semitism
is a degenerate fiction, a myth; and *Lear* is a fiction. Myth
operates within the diagrams of ritual, which presupposes
total and adequate explanations of things as they are and
were; it is a sequence of radically unchangeable gestures.
Fictions are for finding things out, and they change as the
needs of sense-making change. Myths are the agents of
stability, fictions the agents of change. Myths call for absolute, fictions for conditional assent. Myths make sense in
terms of a lost order of time, *illud tempus* as Eliade calls
it; fictions, if successful, make sense of the here and now,
hoc tempus. It may be that treating literary fictions as
myths sounds good just now, but as Marianne Moore so
rightly said of poems, 'these things are important not because a / high-sounding interpretation can be put upon
them but because they are / useful.'

On Vaihinger's view, the fictional *as if* is distinguished
also from hypothesis because it is not in question that at
the end of the finding-out process it will be dropped. In
some ways this is obviously true of the literary fictions. We
are never in danger of thinking that the death of King

Lear, which explains so much, is *true*. To the statement
that he died thus and thus—speaking these words over
Cordelia's body, calling for a looking-glass, fumbling with
a button—we make an experimental assent. If we make
it well, the gain is that we shall never quite resume the
posture towards life and death that we formerly held. Of
course it may be said that in changing ourselves we have,
in the best possible indirect way, changed the world.

So my suggestion is that literary fictions belong to Vaihinger's category of 'the consciously false.' They are not
subject, like hypotheses, to proof or disconfirmation, only,
if they come to lose their operational effectiveness, to neglect. They are then thrown, in Stevens's figure, on to the
'dump'— 'to sit among mattresses of the dead.' In this they
resemble the fictions of science, mathematics, and law, and
differ from those of theology only because religious fictions
are harder to free from the mythical 'deposit.' I see no
reason why we cannot apply to literary fictions what Vaihinger says of fictions in general, that they 'are mental
structures. The psyche weaves this or that thought out of
itself; for the mind is invention; under the compulsion of
necessity, stimulated by the outer world, it discovers the
store of contrivances hidden within itself. The organism
finds itself in a world of contradictory sensations, it is
exposed to the assaults of a hostile world, and in order to
preserve itself is forced to seek every possible means of
assistance.' He distinguishes many different types of fiction:
the paradigmatic, for example, which includes Utopias,
and we may add apocalypses; the legal, where the fiction
has a function in equity (as when a court may deem that
a wife who died at the same instant as, or even some time
later than her husband, pre-deceased him, so as to obviate

an inequitable double payment of estate duties; or as
when, after a certain lapse of time, after receipt, one is
presumed to have accepted delivery of a postal packet);
the fictive zero-cases of mathematics; the fictions of the
thing-in-itself, or of causality; and what Vaihinger calls,
in words remembered by Stevens, 'the last and greatest
fiction,' 'the fiction of an Absolute.' If we forget that fictions are fictive we regress to myth (as when the Neo-
Platonists forgot the fictiveness of Plato's fictions and Professor Frye forgets the fictiveness of *all* fictions). This is as
if we were to believe, because of the grace of the court,
that by an immutable dispensation it always happens that
when a husband and wife are involved in a car crash the
wife dies first, though in ordinary life we may 'displace'
or 'ironize' this basic truth. What Vaihinger calls 'reunion
with reality' and I call 'making sense' or 'making human
sense' is something that literature achieves only so long
as we remember the status of fictions. They are not myths,
and they are not hypotheses; you neither rearrange the
world to suit them, nor test them by experiment, for instance in gas-chambers.

When Vaihinger had to deal with the situation that
arises when men make fictions apparently too elaborate
and ingenious to be explained simply in terms of survival
in a hostile environment (more splendid than seems proper
merely to the mitigation of 'poverty') he made up his Law
of Preponderance of Means over End. We can do without
this, but need to remember not only that we have what
Bergson called a *fonction fabulatrice,* but that we do set
ourselves problems of the kind that would presumably not
arise as a matter of simple biological necessity. When
Nietzsche asked, 'why might not the world *which concerns*

us be a fiction?' he was imagining a very large degree of
human curiosity.

> Meanwhile the mind, from pleasure less,
> Withdraws into its happiness—

but having reached that point it does not cease to produce
fictions beyond necessity:

> it creates, transcending these,
> Far other worlds and other seas.

There are the green thoughts of fantasy, concerned not
only with providing each kind with some convenient mental equivalent but projecting the desires of the mind on to
reality. When the fictions change, therefore, the world
changes in step with them. This is what the poet meant
when he said that modern poetry was 'the act of finding /
What will suffice.' He adds that this used to be easier than
it is now, because 'the scene was set' — we had our paradigmatic fictions, which he calls 'Romantic tenements of
rose and ice.' These no longer serve, and the fiction of the
modern poet must 'speak words in the ear, / The deli-
catest ear of the mind, repeat, / Exactly, that which it
wants to hear . . .' The satisfactions required are too subtle
for the paradigms; but the poem needs to provide them.
'It must be the finding of a satisfaction, and may / Be of
a man skating, a woman dancing, a woman / Combing.'
It has moved, if you like, under the pressure of the Law
of Preponderance of Means over End, away from the paradigm with its simpler biological function; it is a subtler
matter now that utopia or apocalypse or tragedy. Those
Noble Riders have come to look rigid, a bit absurd, as the
same poet remarks.

Nor is it only in literary fictions that the satisfactions,

especially the satisfactions of sceptical clerks, grow more
devious and refined. The recognition, now commonplace,
that the writing of history involves the use of regulative
fictions, is part of the same process. World history, the
imposition of a plot on time, is a substitute for myth, and
the substitution of anti-historicist criticism for it is another
step in the direction of harder satisfactions, in the clerkly
rejection of romantic tenements. There is no history, says
Karl Popper, only histories; an insight in which he was
anticipated by novelists, who wrote Histories (of, say, Tom
Jones, or of the Life of Opinions of Tristram Shandy) in
a period of paradigmatic historiography, as expounded by
Carl Becker in his lectures called *The Heavenly City of
the Eighteenth-Century Philosophers.* The decline of paradigmatic history, and our growing consciousness of historiography's irreducible element of fiction, are, like the sophistication of literary plotting, contributions to what
Wilde called 'the decay of lying.' We fall into 'careless
habits of accuracy.' We know that if we want to find out
about ourselves, make sense, we must avoid the regress
into myth which has deceived poet, historian, and critic.
Our satisfactions will be hard to find.

And yet, it is clear, this is an exaggerated statement of
the case. The paradigms do survive, somehow. If there was
a time when, in Stevens's words, 'the scene was set,' it must
be allowed that is has not yet been finally and totally
struck. The survival of the paradigms is as much our business as their erosion. For that reason it is time to look more
closely at them.

Now presumably it is true, in spite of all possible cultural and historical variations, that the paradigm will

correspond, the more fully as one approaches a condition of absolute simplicity, to some basic human 'set,' biological or psychological. Right down at the root, they must correspond to a basic human need, they must make sense, give comfort. This root may be very primitive; the cultural differentiations must begin pretty far down. It may be that linguistic differentiae, which go very deep, reflect radically different styles of questions asked about the world. But on the other hand it has to be remembered that we know of no cultural group with whom communication is impossible, as a totally different attitude to time, or of course a totally different kind of time, would make it. At some very low level, we all share certain fictions about time, and they testify to the continuity of what is called human nature, however conscious some, as against others, may become of the fictive quality of these fictions.

It seems to follow that we shall learn more concerning the sense-making paradigms, relative to time, from experimental psychologists than from scientists or philosophers, and more from St. Augustine than from Kant or Einstein, because St. Augustine studies time as the soul's necessary self-extension before and after the critical moment upon which he reflects. We shall learn more from Piaget, from studies of such disorders as *déjà vu*, eidetic imagery, the Korsakoff syndrome, than from the learned investigators of time's arrow, or, on the other hand, from the mythic archetypes.

Let us take a very simple example, the ticking of a clock. We ask what it *says:* and we agree that it says *tick-tock*. By this fiction we humanize it, make it talk our language. Of course, it is we who provide the fictional difference between the two sounds; *tick* is our word for a physical beginning, *tock* our word for an end. We say they differ. What enables them to be different is a special kind of middle. We can perceive a duration only when it is organized. It can be shown by experiment that subjects who listen to rhythmic structures such as *tick-tock,* repeated identically, 'can reproduce the intervals within the structure accurately, but they cannot grasp spontaneously the interval between the rhythmic groups,' that is, between *tock* and *tick,* even when this remains constant. The first interval is organized and limited, the second not. According to Paul Fraisse the *tock-tick* gap is analogous to the role of the 'ground' in spatial perception; each is characterized by a lack of form, against which the illusory organizations of shape and rhythm are perceived in the spatial or temporal object. The fact that we call the second of the two related sounds *tock* is evidence that we use fictions to enable the end to confer organization and form on the temporal structure. The interval between the two sounds, between *tick* and *tock* is now charged with significant duration. The clock's *tick-tock* I take to be a model of what we call a plot, an organization that humanizes time by giving it form; and the interval between *tock* and *tick* represents purely successive, disorganized time of the sort that we need to humanize. Later I shall be asking whether, when *tick-tock* seems altogether too easily fictional, we do not produce plots containing a good deal of *tock-tick;* such a plot is that of *Ulysses.*

Tick is a humble genesis, *tock* a feeble apocalypse; and *tick-tock* is in any case not much of a plot. We need much larger ones and much more complicated ones if we persist in finding 'what will suffice.' And what happens if the organization is much more complex than *tick-tock?* Suppose, for instance, that it is a thousand-page novel. Then it obviously will not lie within what is called our 'temporal horizon'; to maintain the experience of organization we shall need many more fictional devices. And although they will essentially be of the same kind as calling the second of those two related sounds *tock,* they will obviously be more resourceful and elaborate. They have to defeat the tendency of the interval between *tick* and *tock* to empty itself; to maintain within that interval following *tick* a lively expectation of *tock,* and a sense that however remote *tock* may be, all that happens happens as if *tock* were certainly following. All such plotting presupposes and requires that an end will bestow upon the whole duration and meaning. To put it another way, the interval must be purged of simple chronicity, of the emptiness of *tock-tick,* humanly uninteresting successiveness. It is required to be a significant season, *kairos* poised between beginning and end. It has to be, on a scale much greater than that which concerns the psychologists, an instance of what they call 'temporal integration'—our way of bundling together perception of the present, memory of the past, and expectation of the future, in a common organization. Within this organization that which was conceived of as simply successive becomes charged with past and future: what was *chronos* becomes *kairos.* This is the time of the novelist, a transformation of mere successiveness which has been likened, by writers as different as Forster and Musil, to the experience of love, the erotic consciousness which makes divinely satisfactory sense out of the commonplace person.

As I intend to use this distinction again, I had better be plain about what I mean by the Greek words, *chronos* and *kairos.* Broadly speaking my usage is derived from the

theologians who have developed this distinction in various
ways, notably Oscar Cullmann in *Christ and Time,* and
John Marsh in *The Fulness of Time.* The distinction has
been familiar in a general way for a good many years, having been given currency by Brabant's *Time and Eternity
in Christian Thought,* of 1937. Tillich uses *kairos* idiosyn-
cratically, but basically he means by it 'moment of crisis,'
or, more obscurely, 'the fate of time'; in any case he has
firmly associated it with a specifically modern sense of living in an epoch when 'the foundations of life quake beneath our feet.' The notion recurs continually in modern
thinking; one instance is Jaspers's 'boundary-situation,'
which has to do with personal crisis—death, suffering, guilt
—in relation to the data which constitute its historical
determination. But Cullmann and Marsh are seeking to
use the words *kairos* and *chronos* in their historical, biblical senses: *chronos* is 'passing time' or 'waiting time'—
that which, according to Revelation, 'shall be no more'—
and *kairos* is the season, a point in time filled with significance, charged with a meaning derived from its relation
to the end.

You can see that this is a very radical distinction. The
Greeks, as Mr. Lampert observes, thought that even the
gods could not change the past; but Christ did change it,
rewrote it, and in a new way fulfilled it. In the same way
the End changes all, and produces, in what in relation to
it is the past, these seasons, *kairoi,* historical moments of
intemporal significance. The divine plot is the pattern of
kairoi in relation to the End. Not only the Greeks but the
Hebrews lacked this antithesis; for Hebrew, according to
Marsh, had no word for *chronos,* and so no contrast between time which is simply 'one damn thing after another'

and time as concentrated in *kairoi*. It is the New Testament that lays the foundation for both the modern sense of epoch (it is very conscious of existing in an overlap of *aiones*) and the modern distinction between times: the coming of God's time *(kairos),* the fulfilling of the time *(kairos*—Mark i.15), the signs of the times (Matt. xvi.2,3) as against passing time, *chronos.* The notion of fulfilment is essential; the *kairos* transforms the past, validates Old Testament types and prophecies, establishes concord with origins as well as ends. The *chronos–kairos* distinction is therefore relevant to the typological interests of some modern theologians, and also some modern literary critics; Miss Helen Gardner has attacked both classes, justly in my view, for their typological obsessions, which, she thinks, diminish the force and actuality of the Gospels, as they do of secular literature. The attractiveness of the types must in the end be explained in terms of the service they do to the man who senses his position in the middest, desiring these moments of significance which harmonize origin and end.

It would be wrong not to allude, at this point, to a critic of such distinctions, Professor James T. Barr. He examines the work of Cullman, Marsh, J.A.T. Robinson, and others, calling it characteristic of modern biblical theology 'at its best' but arguing that all these scholars misinterpret the language of the Bible. The *chronos–kairos* distinction is simply not in the language of the New Testament. In Galatians 4.4. the words translated as 'the fulness of the time' are *pleroma tou chronou,* though Mark 1.15, already quoted, has *peplerotai ho kairos,* 'the time is fulfilled.' In Acts 1.7 and I. Thess. 5.1 the terms seem not to be differentiated: *hoi chronoi kai hoi kairoi,* which the Authorized Version translates 'the times and the seasons.' Also, says

Barr, the Old Testament shows much more interest in passing-time, chronicity, than these scholars have suggested. In the New Testament, *kairos* and *chronos* can be opposed, but are sometimes interchangeable; perhaps *kairos* leans, as Augustine thought, towards 'critical time'; *chronos* is more quantitative. But we cannot, according to Barr, have a '*kairos* concept,' and to say, as G. A. F. Knight does, that "the story of the people of God is full of crises, *kairoi*, 'decisive moments,'" is not to use the word in a biblical sense at all.

Mr. Barr's authoritative book contains much more destructive criticism than this suggests. Among other things, it discourages too easy acceptance of sharp distinctions between Christian rectilinearity and Greek cyclism. But the main issue here is that Barr makes it impossible for anybody who is not willing to engage him on his own lexical terms to doubt that Marsh's distinction, which I have used, can have any very certain validity. It is overstated. The best one can hope for is that the words, in New Testament Greek, maintain a certain polarity, though they also shade off into one another—they cover the same ground as the word 'time' does in *Macbeth*. It makes one think of Wittgenstein's famous passage on games. 'Back to the rough ground! Look and see!' Our notion of time includes, among much else, *kairos, chronos,* and *aion*. Even if their lexical methods are faulty, it is important that these modern theologians *want* these words to mean involved distinctions of the sort I have discussed. They play, as Wittgenstein might have said, and make up the rules as they go along. These rules are attractive; and they are so because we need, for our obscure cultural ends, to observe distinctions between mere chronicity and times

which are concordant and full. Hence our use, for our own
game, of *chronos, kairos,* and also *pleroma.*

We can use this kind of language to distinguish between
what we *feel* is happening in a fiction when mere successiveness, which we *feel* to be the chief characteristic in the
ordinary going-on of time, is purged by the establishment
of a significant relation between the moment and a remote
origin and end, a concord of past, present, and future—
three dreams which, as Augustine said, cross in our minds,
as in the present of things past, the present of things present, and the present of things future. Normally we associate 'reality' with *chronos,* and a fiction which entirely
ignored this association we might think unserious or silly
or mad; only the unconscious is intemporal, and the illusion that the world can be made to satisfy the unconscious
is an illusion without a future.

Yet in every plot there is an escape from chronicity, and
so, in some measure, a deviation from this norm of 'reality.' When we read a novel we are, in a way, allowing ourselves to behave as young children do when they think of
all the past as 'yesterday,' or like members of primitive
cargo-cults when they speak of the arrival of Jesus a couple
of generations back as a guarantee of another good cargo
in the near future. Our past is brief, organized by our
desire for satisfaction, and simply related to our future.
But there is a pattern of expectation improper to maturity.
Having compared the novel-reader with an infant and a
primitive, one can go further and compare him with a
psychopath; and this I shall shortly be doing. But all I
want to say at present is that any novel, however 'realistic,'
involves some degree of alienation from 'reality.' You can
see the difficulty Fielding, for example, felt about this, at

the very beginning of the serious novel; he felt he had to reject the Richardsonian method of novels by epistolary correspondences, although this made sure that in the midst of voluminous detail intended to ensure realism, everything became *kairios* by virtue of the way in which letters coincided with critical moments. Fielding preferred to assume the right to convert one kind of time into another exactly as he pleased; if it is proper that a long period of time should elapse without producing anything notable, he will, he says, leave it 'totally unobserved.' In other words, Fielding allows the narrator to dispense with chronicity when he chooses, but feels it necessary to explain what he is doing. With some differences, he does what is done in the Greek romances. In fact Richardson is the more modern, and Fielding worries about it. His book, he says, is a 'history,' not a 'life'; and history isn't chronicle, ignores whatever is not concordant. *The History of Tom Jones* has nevertheless a critical 'middle,' the scene at Upton, in which the delayed arrivals, the split-second timing, as we now say, belong to the *kairos* of farce rather than to the *chronos* of reality; and he is especially proud of the concords he establishes with origins and ends in this passage. In short, he is, and would have been happy to hear it, of the family of Don Quixote, tilting with a hopeless chivalry against the dull windmills of a time-bound reality. All novelists must do so; but it is important that the great ones retreat from reality less perfunctorily than the authors of novelettes and detective stories.

Georges Poulet argues that medieval men did not distinguish as we do between existence and duration; one can only say that they were very lucky, and less in need than we are of fictions relating to time—the kind that con-

fer significance on the interval between *tick* and *tock*. For
his medieval men, it seems, this significance was a simple
property of the interval. We have to provide it. We still
need the fullness of it, the *pleroma;* and it is our insatiable
interest in the future (towards which we are biologically
orientated) that makes it necessary for us to relate to the
past, and to the moment in the middle, by plots: by which
I mean not only concordant imaginary incidents, but all
the other, perhaps subtler, concords that can be arranged
in a narrative. Such concords can easily be called 'time-
defeating,' but the objection to that word is that it leads
directly to the questionable critical practice of calling literary structures *spatial*. This is a critical fiction which has
regressed into a myth because it was not discarded at the
right moment in the argument. 'Time-redeeming' is a
better word, perhaps.

One implication of this argument is that the 'virtual'
time of books—to use Mrs. Langer's word—is a kind of
man-centred model of world-time. And books are indeed
world-models. St. Augustine found that the best model he
could find for our experience of past, present, and future
was the recitation of a psalm. Thus he anticipated all the
modern critics who wonder how it can be that a book can
simultaneously be present like a picture (though in a way
a picture has also to be recited) and yet extended in time.
Curtius testifies to the durability of the book as a world-
model in the Middle Ages. Like the ziggurat, the Byzan-
tine church, and most of all like the Gothic cathedral, it
is a perpetual testimony to the set of our demands on the
world. If the ziggurat is a topocosm, the book is a biblio-
cosm. We can distribute our fictions in time as well as in
space, which is why we must avoid an easy translation from

the one to the other. E. H. Gombrich has recently been
talking about the relevance of the great eleventh chapter
of Augustine's *Confessions,* to which I have already referred, and finding in it the seeds of modern psychological
speculation about the action of memory. There is the
matter of mere physiological persistence—which makes
television possible. There is 'immediate memory,' or 'primary retention,' the registration of impressions we fail to
'take in,' but can recover a little later by introspection;
and there is, finally, a kind of forward memory, familiar
from spoonerisms and typing errors which are caused by
anticipation, the mind working on an expected future.
The second of these memories—registration of what we
fail to 'take in'—is an essential tool of narrative fiction. It
is familiar from the 'double-take' of the music-hall, and
many literary kinds, from poems which catch up words
and ideas into new significance, to complicated plots like
that of *Tom Jones,* depend on it. Aristotle's notion of the
best possible plot is a double-take. There is a sense in
which *Macbeth* is an enormous dramatic extension of the
double-take, for it is based on an initial deviation of attention which causes a temporal gap between the original
apprehension of what the situation signifies and the final
understanding that its significance was other. The third
kind of memory is what enables writers to use the *peripeteia,* a falsification of expectation, so that the end comes
as expected, but not in the manner expected.

Gombrich's argument is that we ignore these facts when
we make a sharp *a priori* distinction between time and
space; that in time our minds work in fashions that are
not wholly and simply successive, while in spatial appreci-
ations—as when one looks at a painting—there is a temporal

element; one 'scans' the picture and could not do so without retinal persistence; one remembers what has passed,
and has expectations about what is to come. These are
matters on which he has previously spoken in *Art and
Illusion*. I quote him in support of a revaluation of the
element of temporal structure, memory, and expectation,
as against the tendency to reduce our bibliocosms to
merely spatial order. It seems obvious that in the experience of literature we use temporal expectation—a 'mental
set,' as Gombrich puts it, which is 'a state of readiness to
start projecting.' We remember that in Stevens the 'angel
of reality' gives us the power 'to see the earth again /
Cleared of its stiff and stubborn, man-locked set'; and that
he aims at 'meanings said / By repetition of half-meanings'
—by using the second kind of memory to play upon the
expectations created by the third.

So we may call books fictive models of the temporal
world. They will be humanly serviceable as models only
if they pay adequate respect to what we think of as 'real'
time, the chronicity of the waking moment. If we are
normal we can guess the time—we can guess how long ago
the lecture began, and also how long we shall have to wait
for some desire to be gratified, for example, that the lecture should end. (It is, as a matter of fact, harder for the
lecturer to do this: he is in love with what he is saying, or
should be. A good illustration of his lapse into a terrible
loveless chronicity is provided by Jim's lecture in Kingsley
Amis's novel; he assembles it in discrete temporal pieces,
minute by painful minute.)

But even outside literature other needs, in conflict with
reality, can dispose us to behave in defiance of this normality. Under certain drugs the 'specious present' is indefi-

nitely lengthened. Schizophrenics can lose contact with
'real' time, and undergo what has been called 'a transformation of the present into eternity.' The ability to wait
for the gratification of a desire is measurably less in children and in old people than in the mature; it is very low
in the emotionally disturbed, especially in juvenile delin-
quents. And as readers we do seem to partake of some of
these abnormally acute appetites. We hunger for ends and
for crises. 'Is this the promis'd end?' we ask with Kent in
Lear; if not, we require that it be an image of it. Perhaps
in a plot which depends on those subtle repetitions which
E. M. Forster calls 'rhythms,' we have a sophisticated analogue of *déjà vu,* a condition of pathological origin. In
granting the narrator something like total recall we again
move away from normality into pathology. It is not merely,
as I suggested, that we are like children; we are like some
abnormal children, such as the autistic, who invent the
most arbitrary and painful fictions. It seems that there is
in narrative an atavism of our temporal attitudes, modified
always by a refusal quite to give up our 'realism' about
time; so that a modern novel has to hold some kind of
balance between the two. The clock striking at the end of
Marlowe's *Faustus* is an impressive intrusion of successive
time upon a great crisis; but a modern novelist would find
some disparity in the fact that Faustus gets through only
fifty lines of verse between eleven and twelve o'clock.

But of course temporal realism, and also the high organization of the *tick-tock* interval, belong to the modern
novel, not to Homer or Greek romance or Elizabethan
drama before Shakespeare. The history of the novel shows
an increasing attention to such organization, and to the
balance of regressive pleasure and the sense of reality. In

other words, because the form requires that the realism of
the ego, and the desires of the lower mind, be simultaneously satisfied, the novel has to modify the paradigms—
organize extensive middles in concordance with remote
origins and predictable ends—in such a way as to preserve
its difference from dreaming or other fantasy gratifications.

These are questions of cultural modification. A desire to
use the past denotes, we are told, an evolutionary phase
already quite advanced. To find patterns in historical time
—a time free of the repetitions of ritual, and indifferent
to the ecstasies of the shāman—is yet another stage. And
the assumption or understanding that finding such patterns is a purely anthropocentric activity belongs to a third
phase. We are still not quite easy with it. Much of our
thinking still belongs to the second phase, when history,
historiographical plot-making, did the work of ritual or
tradition. 'The thread of historical continuity,' as Hannah
Arendt notices, 'was the first substitute for tradition; by
means of it the overwhelming mass of the most divergent
values, the most contradictory thoughts and conflicting
authorities . . . we reduced to a unilinear, dialectically consistent development.' History, so considered, is a fictive
substitute for authority and tradition, a maker of concords
between past, present, and future, a provider of significance to mere chronicity. Everything is relevant if its relevance can be invented, even the scattered informations of
the morning newspaper. The novel imitates historiography
in this: anything can take its important place in the concord, a beerpull in a Joycean pub, a long-legged Indian
wasp. The merely successive character of events has been
exorcised; the synthesizing consciousness has done its work.
Order, as Giovanni Gentile puts it of historiography, 'has

ceased to be a succession and become an inter-connexion
of parts all mutually implied and conditioned in the
whole.'

But the third stage is marked by an understanding that
this play of consciousness over history, this plot making,
may relieve us of time's burden only by defying our sense
of reality. To be really free of time we should have, perhaps, to be totally unconscious, or in some other way indifferent to what we normally call real. 'What Kant took to
be the necessary schemata of reality,' says a modern Freudian, 'are really only the necessary schemata of repression.'
And an experimental psychologist adds that 'a sense of
time can only exist where there is submission to reality.'
To see everything as out of mere succession is to behave
like a man drugged or insane. Literature and history, as
we know them, are not like that; they must submit, be
repressed. It is characteristic of the stage we are now at,
I think, that the question of how far this submission ought
to go—or, to put it the other way, how far one may culti-
vate fictional patterns or paradigms—is one which is de-
bated, under various forms, by existentialist philosophers,
by novelists and anti-novelists, by all who condemn the
myths of historiography. It is a debate of fundamental interest, I think, and I shall discuss it in my fifth talk.

Certainly, it seems, there must, even when we have
achieved a modern degree of clerical scepticism, be some
submission to the fictive patterns. For one thing, a systematic submission of this kind is almost another way of describing what we call 'form.' 'An inter-connexion of parts
all mutually implied'; a duration (rather than a space)
organizing the moment in terms of the end, giving meaning to the interval between *tick* and *tock* because we hu-

manly do not want it to be an indeterminate interval between the *tick* of birth and the *tock* of death. That is a
way of speaking in temporal terms of literary form. One
thinks again of the Bible: of a beginning and an end (denied by the physicist Aristotle to the world) but humanly
acceptable (and allowed by him to plots). Revelation, which
epitomizes the Bible, puts our fate into a book, and calls
it the book of life, which is the holy city. Revelation answers the command, 'write the things which thou hast
seen, and the things which are, and the things which shall
be hereafter'—'what is past and passing and to come'—and
the command to make these things interdependent. Our
novels do likewise. Biology and cultural adaptation require it; the End is a fact of life and a fact of the imagination, working out from the middle, the human crisis.
As the theologians say, we 'live from the End,' even if the
world should be endless. We need ends and *kairoi* and the
pleroma, even now when the history of the world has so
terribly and so untidily expanded its endless successiveness.
We re-create the horizons we have abolished, the structures
that have collapsed; and we do so in terms of the old patterns, adapting them to our new worlds. Ends, for example,
become a matter of images, figures for what does not exist
except humanly. Our stories must recognize mere successiveness but not be merely successive; *Ulysses*, for example,
may be said to unite the irreducible *chronos* of Dublin
with the irreducible *kairoi* of Homer. In the middest, we
look for a fullness of time, for beginning, middle, and end
in concord.

For concord or consonance really is the root of the matter, even in a world which thinks it can only be a fiction.
The theologians revive typology, and are followed by the

literary critics. We seek to repeat the performance of the New Testament, a book which rewrites and requites another book and achieves harmony with it rather than questioning its truth. One of the seminal remarks of modern literary thought was Eliot's observation that in the timeless order of literature this process is continued. Thus we secularize the principle which recurs from the New Testament through Alexandrian allegory and Renaissance Neo-Platonism to our own time. We achieve our secular concords of past and present and future, modifying the past and allowing for the future without falsifying our own moment of crisis. We need, and provide, fictions of concord.

I think one can speak of specifically modern concord-fictions, and say that what they have in common is the practice of treating the past (and the future) as a special case of the present. I'll try to explain this by referring to a concord-fiction which has its origin not in theology or literature but in physics. It is a fiction which not only uses the past as a special case but is designed to relate events that appear to be discrete and humanly inexplicable to an acceptable human pattern. It is the so-called Principle of Complementarity.

This Principle arose from a precise scientific need. Light behaves in such a way that you can think of it in terms of waves, and it behaves also so that you can think of it in terms of particles; it proved possible, mathematically, to develop a single set of equations to cover both wave and particle effects, but outside mathematics you could only speak of them as being 'complementary.' The implications of this within physics, which are fortunately not my business, are that observations in themselves only partially true can be so reconciled by mathematical formalism that theoretical prediction and empirical observation are brought into congruence. But this new concord raises the question of what to do with the old ones, now discredited. The new one depends upon a new appraisal of probability; an interest in systems with small quantum numbers makes it necessary to deal with uncertainty as if it were of the world rather than of the human mind; in classical physics uncertainty is an epistemological issue, not part of the nature of things to be dealt with by sophisticated mathematical procedures.

This being so, classical physics is either wrong, or there is a natural discontinuity between large and small systems. Neither of these answers is agreeable; classical physics works over a vast area, and nature does not, we say, make leaps. So this either-or is rejected; instead of saying the older physics is wrong, Heisenberg calls it a special case of modern physics. Classical mechanics is a special case of quantum mechanics, classical logic of quantum logic, and so on. What appeared to be law in the past was law expressed in a manner consistent with the observational situation at the time; with certain qualifications (it works only for large quantum numbers) it is still lawful, though not in accord with the facts. In this way the past is included in, is complementary with, the present.

Now it is clear that if the interests of the scientists were purely pragmatic they would not bother about this kind of complementarity, but use the concept in a simple operational way, as a discursive equivalent for an ingenious bit of mathematics. Their refusal to do this escalates complementarity into a Principle. Heisenberg himself says that classical and quantum physics are alike human responses to nature, and compares them with different styles of art: 'the style arises out of the interplay between the world and ourselves . . . both science and art form in the course of the centuries a human language by which we can speak of the more remote parts of reality.' Modern art, like modern science, can establish complementary relations with discredited fictional systems: as Newtonian mechanics is to quantum mechanics, so *King Lear* is to *Endgame*.

More extreme applications of the Principle are associated with the name of Nils Bohr. Obstinate discords of other kinds than wave and particle might be resolved in the same way. He will establish complementarity between, say, mechanism and vitalism in biology, East and West in politics, love and justice in communal life. It is true that in some situations we cannot distinguish between a fact and our knowledge of the fact, which is what the physicists say about their subatomic observations; so it seems to make sense for Heisenberg to say that 'the situation of complementarity is not confined to the atomic world alone.' 'We meet it,' he goes on, 'when we reflect about a decision, or when we have the choice between enjoying music and analyzing its structure.' But here, I think, we are already reaching the point where we are enjoying complementarity for its own sake. Northrop, in his introduction to the translation of Heisenberg's book, points to the dangers of 'playing fast and loose with the law of contradiction, in the name of complementarity,' and there is a sharper critique in Bridgman's *The Way Things Are*. Nevertheless, the Principle is proving very attractive, for example to exponents of Jung; Dr. von Franz has recently been saying that the relationship between consciousness and unconscious-

ness is a complementarity analogous to that between wave
and particle in physics.

In the end one can imagine the Principle being used
to establish a consonance between what is so and what is
not so; propositions may even yet be true and false at the
same time. But whatever we may think of these extensions
of the Principle—whether there is a principle that applies
to waves and particles, love and justice, enjoyment and
analysis, conscious and unconscious—it remains clear that
this is an interesting example of the way in which an operationalist fiction outgrows its immediate purpose. Its object can be generalized as being the establishment of concord between the world of normal thought and that of
nuclear physics, between observations originally hard to
categorize and somewhat disquieting, and an order acceptable to our mental set. Now it is extended to cover other
disquieting gaps, intervals in thought and experience; it
is doing a job analogous to that of literary fictions. It is,
in short, what I call a concord-fiction. Bohr is really doing
what the Stoic allegorists did to close the gap between
their world and Homer's, or what St. Augustine did when
he explained, against the evidence, the concord of the
canonical scriptures. The dissonances as well as the harmonies have to be made concordant by means of some
ultimate complementarity. Later biblical scholarship has
sought different explanations, and more sophisticated concords; but the motive is the same, however the methods
may differ. An epoch, as Einstein remarked, is the instru-
ments of its research. Stoic physics, biblical typology,
Copenhagen quantum theory, are all different, but all use
concord-fictions and assert complementarities.

Such fictions meet a need. They seem to do what Bacon

said poetry could: 'give some show of satisfaction to the mind, wherein the nature of things doth seem to deny it.' Literary fictions (Bacon's 'poetry') do likewise. One consequence is that they change, for the same reason that patristic allegory is not the same thing, though it may be essentially the same *kind* of thing, as the physicists' Principle of Complementarity. The show of satisfaction will only serve when there seems to be a degree of real compliance with reality as we, from time to time, imagine it. Thus we might imagine a constant value for the irreconcileable observations of the reason and the imagination, the one immersed in *chronos,* the other in *kairos;* but the proportions vary indeterminably. Or, when we find 'what will suffice,' the element of what I have called the paradigmatic will vary. We measure and order time with our fictions; but time seems, in reality, to be ever more diverse and less and less subject to any uniform system of measurement. Thus we think of the past in very different timescales, according to what we are doing; the time of the art-historian is different from that of the geologist, that of the football coach from the anthropologist's. There is a time of clocks, a time of radioactive carbon, a time even of linguistic change, as in lexicostatics. None of these is the same as the 'structural' or 'family' time of sociology. George Kubler in his book *The Shape of Time* distinguished between 'absolute' and 'systematic' age, a hierarchy of durations from that of the coral reef to that of the solar year. Our ways of filling the interval between the *tick* and *tock* must grow more difficult and more self-critical, as well as more various; the need we continue to feel is a need of concord, and we supply it by increasingly varied concord-fictions. They change as the reality from which we, in the middest, seek a show of satisfaction, changes; because 'times change.' The fictions by which we seek to find 'what will suffice' change also. They change because we no longer live in a world with an historical *tick* which will certainly be consummated by a definitive *tock*. And among all the other changing fictions, literary fictions take their place. They find out about the changing world on our behalf; they arrange our complementarities. They do this, for some of us, perhaps better than history, perhaps better than theology, largely because they are consciously false; but the way to understand their development is to see how they are related to those other fictional systems. It is not that we are connoisseurs of chaos, but that we are surrounded by it, and equipped for co-existence with it only by our fictive powers. This may, in the absence of a supreme fiction or the possibility of it, be a hard fate; which is why the poet of that fiction is compelled to say

> From this the poem springs: that we live in a place
> That is not our own, and much more, nor ourselves
> And hard it is, in spite of blazoned days.

It is also why literary fictions die, lose their explanatory force; and why fictions which do not change never even begin to live but sink into myths and satisfy nobody but critics who lack the critic's first qualification, a scepticism, an interest in things as they are, in inhuman reality as well as in human justice.

III

True then is it that man is purged by none but the 'beginning,'
but this 'beginning' is by them too variably taken.

ST. AUGUSTINE

The generations of men run on in the tide of Time,
But leave their destin'd lineaments permanent for ever and ever.

BLAKE

World Without End or Beginning

It is worth remembering that the rise of what we call literary fiction happened at a time when the revealed, authenticated account of the beginning was losing its authority. Now that changes in things as they are change beginnings to make them fit, beginnings have lost their mythical rigidity. There are, it is true, modern attempts to restore this rigidity. But on the whole there is a correlation between subtlety and variety in our fictions and remoteness and doubtfulness about ends and origins. There is a necessary relation between the fictions by which we order our world and the increasing complexity of what we take to be the 'real' history of that world.

I propose in this talk to ask some questions about an early and very interesting example of this relation. There was a long-established opinion that the beginning was as described in Genesis, and that the end is to be as obscurely predicted in Revelation. But what if this came to seem doubtful? Supposing reason proved capable of a quite different account of the matter, an account contradicting that of faith? On the argument of these talks so far as they have gone, you would expect two developments: there should be generated fictions of concord between the old

and the new explanations; and there should be consequen-
tial changes in fictive accounts of the world. And of course
I should not be troubling you with all this if I did not
think that such developments occurred.

The changes to which I refer came with a new wave of
Greek influence on Christian philosophy. The provision
of accommodations between Greek and Hebrew thought
is an old story, and a story of concord-fictions—necessary,
as Berdyaev says, because to the Greeks the world was a
cosmos, but to the Hebrews a history. But this is too enormous a tract in the history of ideas for me to wander in.
I shall make do with my single illustration, and speak of
what happened in the thirteenth century when Christian
philosophers grappled with the view of the Aristotelians
that nothing can come of nothing—*ex nihilo nihil fit*—so
that the world must be thought to be eternal.

In the Bible the world is made out of nothing. For the
Aristotelians, however, it is eternal, without beginning or
end. To examine the Aristotelian arguments impartially
one would need to behave as if the Bible might be wrong.
And this was done. The thirteenth-century rediscovery of
Aristotle led to the invention of double-truth. It takes a
good deal of sophistication to do what certain philosophers
then did, namely, to pursue with vigour rational enquiries
the validity of which one is obliged to deny. And the
eternity of the world was, of course, more than a question
in a scholarly game. It called into question all that might
seem ragged and implausible in the usual accounts of the
temporal structure of the world, the relation of time to
eternity (certainly untidy and discordant compared with
the Neo-Platonic version) and of heaven to hell.

St. Augustine, working long before at some of the prob-

lems, came up with a formless matter, intermediate between nothing and something, out of which the world was
made. This, of course, was created out of nothing. Formless, it had the potentiality of form, its privation is its
capacity to receive form. He identifies this capacity with
mutability; creation, for him, is a concept inseparable from
that of mutability, of which time is the mode. The 'seminal
reasons' are the potentialities to be actualized in time.
These seminal forms were later distinguished, by Boethius,
from the Platonic forms of which they were images, but
in time and matter, not in eternity and the mind of God;
in what he called the *nunc movens* and not the *nunc stans*,
where everything has perfect being and not potentiality.
Thus we have a creation of which the law relating to forms
is a law of change and succession, and a Creator whose
realm and forms are changeless and non-successive.

Broadly speaking, this exnihilistic explanation held till
the thirteenth century, when Aristotle and his Arab commentators were brought in. By the 1270s, when with many
other philosophical positions it was condemned, the eternity of the world and the denial of personal immortality
that went with it were well known, and identified especially with Averroes. Albertus Magnus believed the Averroistic position could be disproved by reason, but his
pupil St. Thomas did not; he thought reason could prove
neither creation *ex nihilo* nor an eternal world, saying that
we must believe the former not because of any rational
proof but simply because of revelation. He then saved as
much of Aristotle as was consistent with revelation, defin-
ing matter as pure potentiality, pure privation, upon
which form imposed itself as horse, beetle, or man. What
is 'educed' from the 'potency of matter' is infinitely vari-

able. Men, like everything else, have one form; but it is a
substance, and can subsist independently of matter, and
so the immortality of the soul is saved from Averroistic
attack.

In this way Aquinas saved the Christian origins but substituted an Aristotelian for an Augustinian account of
prime matter. He also needed a new rationale for angels.
The angels could not be pure being, since then they would
be indistinguishable from God; so they must either be allowed to possess materiality, or to be of a third order,
neither matter, with its potentiality, nor pure act, but
immaterial with potentiality. St. Thomas decided that the
latter was the right choice. His angels, though immutable
as to substance, are capable of change by acts of will and
intellect. So they are separated from the corporeal creation,
which is characterized by a distinction between matter and
form, and also from God. They are therefore neither
eternal nor of time. So out of this argument, which is
ultimately an argument about origins, there develops a
third duration, between that of time and eternity. To put
this another way, angels must be 'simple' but not as 'simple'
as God. One answer might be that they had a material element. St. Bonaventure thought so, and, to name a theorist
with whom most of us are more familiar, Milton did, too;
the philosophical and poetic problems this belief set him
are notorious. But Aquinas thought otherwise, as I've said,
and so he had to invent this third order of duration, distinct from time and eternity. Needing to give it a name,
he adopted a word he had heard Albert the Great use.
Perhaps Albert got it from Augustine. Anyway, St. Thomas
called this third order *aevum*.

Aevum, I should add, is by no means the only time-fiction of its kind. It seems quite normal for people to think up first a second kind of time, later perhaps made very sophisticated and called eternity, and it isn't altogether unusual to add a third, as Aquinas did; there are modern instances, for example in Ouspensky and J. B. Priestley. But St. Thomas's fiction is especially interesting and productive.

The formerly absolute distinction between time and eternity in Christian thought—between *nunc movens* with its beginning and end, and *nunc stans*, the perfect possession of endless life—acquired a third intermediate order based on this peculiar betwixt-and-between position of angels. But like the Principle of Complementarity, this concord-fiction soon proved that it had uses outside its immediate context, angelology. Because it served as a means of talking about certain aspects of human experience, it was humanized. It helped one to think about the sense men sometimes have of participating in some order of duration other than that of the *nunc movens*—of being able, as it were, to do all that angels can. Such are those moments which Augustine calls the moments of the soul's attentiveness; less grandly, they are moments of what psychologists call 'temporal integration.' When Augustine recited his psalm he found in it a figure for the integration of past, present, and future which defies successive time. He discovered what is now erroneously referred to as 'spatial form.' He was anticipating what we know of the relation between books and St. Thomas's third order of duration—for in the kind of time known by books a moment has endless perspectives of reality. We feel, in Thomas Mann's words, that 'in their beginning exists their middle and their end, their past invades the present, and

even the most extreme attention to the present is invaded
by concern for the future.' The concept of *aevum* provides
a way of talking about this unusual variety of duration—
neither temporal nor eternal, but, as Aquinas said, participating in both the temporal and the eternal. It does
not abolish time or spatialize it; it co-exists with time, and
is a mode in which things can be perpetual without being
eternal.

We've seen that the concept of *aevum* grew out of a
need to answer certain specific Averroistic doctrines concerning origins. But it appeared quite soon that this *medium inter aeternitatem et tempus* had human uses. It
contains beings (angels) with freedom of choice and immutable substance, in a creation which is in other respects
determined. Although these beings are out of time, their
acts have a before and an after. *Aevum, you might say,
is the time-order of novels. Characters in novels are inde-
pendent of time and succession, but may and usually do
seem to operate in time and succession; the *aevum* co-exists
with temporal events at the moment of occurrence, being,
it was said, like a stick in a river. Brabant believed that
Bergson inherited the notion through Spinoza's *duratio,*
and if this is so there is an historical link between the
aevum and Proust; furthermore this *durée réelle* is, I
think, the real sense of modern 'spatial form,' which is a
figure for the *aevum.*

The word *aevum* was available to the scholastics because
the Vulgate translated the Greek *aion* as *saeculum.* This
left available the true Latin equivalent, *aevum,* for the
new order of time. It appears to be a characteristic of words
for time that they are constantly adapted to new human
uses. *Aion* was used by the Gnostics to mean the time of

a world of becoming. Then, as we have seen, it became
the time of the angels, and then the time of men in certain
postures of attentiveness, and especially the mode of certain
human approaches to perpetuity. The political and juris-
tic employment of the concept has been studied by Ernst
Kantorowicz. The emperor possesses a kind of perpetuity,
his halo signifies the *perennitas* of David's kingdom. His
natural body is subject to time, but his *dignitas* exists perpetually in the *aevum*. In this sense the emperor or king
'never dies'; Rome never dies, but invests Byzantium or
Moscow; the *maiestas populi romani* persists in the nations
of Europe. The doctrine of the King's Two Bodies, says
Kantorowicz, 'camouflaged a problem of continuity' which
became manifest with the reception in the West of Aris-
totelian-Averroist teachings on an eternal world. At the
same time questions of continuity were engaging lawyers;
in Kantorowicz's words, 'some serious change was taking
place within the realm of Time, and in man's relation to
Time.' More properly, a new conceptual tool facilitated
human movement within, and control of, this area of
thought. If the world was not eternal—and the thesis had
been condemned more than once—there was nevertheless
quite recognizably a sort of immortality, a perpetuity, in
certain aspects of human life. The fiction which provided
a duration for angels, and later for the Platonic Ideas,
which were also by some held to reside in the *aevum*, was
brought down to earth and used to reconcile certain discordant observations concerning human life. What of the
kind of time which preserved, as opposed to that which
destroyed?

Aristotle in *De Anima* spoke of man's being-for-ever in
the cycle of life and in his *De Generatione* called the cycle

of generation a sort of second-best eternity ('eternal in the manner that is open to it'). Remembering this idea of Aristotle's, it was possible also to see that human and indeed animal life, considered as a genetic perpetuity, also inhabited this order. Thus was invented an image of endlessness consistent with a temporal end. Historical events might be unique, and given pattern by an end; yet there are perpetuities which defy both the uniqueness and the end. Human society thus took on certain angelic characteristics. In law, for example, corporations became 'immortal species,' and the lawyers themselves recognized that there was a 'similarity between their abstractions and the angelic beings.' The Empire, the People, the legal corporation, the king, would never die, because each was *persona mystica,* a single person in perpetuity; and the entire cycle of created life, with its perpetuation of specific forms, had the same kind of eternity within a non-eternal world. The old Platonic distinction between *athanasia* and *aei einai,* deathlessness and being-for-ever, was given a new fictive shape; men can have the first, but not the second, truly eternal, quality.

This kind of fiction, you will agree, is likely to be reflected in literature. It facilitates a different, more flexible attitude to life as it seems to be when you look at the whole picture from your place in the middest. And I want now to look at some evidence that the fiction of the *aevum* had this effect. First comes a philosophical poet—someone thinking in poetry about the problem itself, the problem of perpetuities in the creation and in human life; and then another poet who will help me to illustrate the effect of the theory rather than its substance.

A sixteenth-century poet, especially one who knew that he ought to be a curious and universal scholar, would possess some notions, perhaps not strictly philosophical, about the origin of the world and its end, the eduction of forms from matter, and the relation of such forms to the higher forms which are the model of the world and have their being in the mind of God. He might well be a poet to brood on those great complementary opposites: the earthly and heavenly cities, unity and multiplicity, light and dark, equity and justice, continuity—as triumphantly exhibited in his own Empress—and ends—as sadly exhibited in his own Empress. Like St. Augustine he will see mutability as the condition of all created things, which are immersed in time. Time, he knows, will have a stop—perhaps, on some of the evidence, quite soon. Yet there is other evidence to suggest that this is not so. It will seem to him, at any rate, that his poem should in part rest on some poetic generalization—some fiction—which reconciles these opposites, and helps to make sense of the discords, ethical, political, legal, and so forth, which, in its completeness, it had to contain.

This may stand as a rough account of Spenser's mood when he worked out the sections of his poem which treat of the Garden of Adonis and the trial of Mutability, the first dealing with the sempiternity of earthly forms, and the second with the dilation of being in these forms under the shadow of a final end. Perhaps the refinements upon, and the substitutes for, Augustine's explanations of the first matter and its potentialities, do not directly concern him; as an allegorist he may think most readily of these potentialities in a quasi-Augustinian way as seeds, seminal

reasons, plants tended in a *seminarium*. But he will distinguish, as his commentators often fail to do, these forms
or *formulae* from the heavenly forms, and allow them the
kind of immortality that is open to them, that of *athanasia*
rather than of *aei einai*. And an obvious place to talk about
them would be in the discussion of love, since without the
agency represented by Venus there would be no eduction
of forms from the prime matter. Elsewhere he would have
to confront the problem of Plato's two kinds of eternity;
the answer to Mutability is that the creation is deathless,
but the last stanzas explain that this is not to grant them
the condition of being-for-ever.

In the Garden of Adonis canto, Spenser is talking about
the *aevum,* the quasi-eternal aspect of the world. When
Venus goes in search of Cupid she leaves 'her heavenly
house, / The house of goodly formes' to do so. From these
forms, we learn, derive the 'shapes select' of the world.
These are lower forms, which have the deathlessness of perpetual succession rather than the being-for-ever of the
higher forms. The meeting of Venus with Phoebe distinguishes their roles; the business of Venus in her pandemic
form is to ensure the immortality of the kinds. Her Garden
has the voluptuousness necessary to ensure this, and is 'the
first seminarie / Of all things that are borne to live and
die / According to their kindes.' Under the eye of Genius,
the 'naked babies' pass out through a golden, and return
through an iron wall. Out there they are clad in 'sinful
mire,' but on their return are replanted, grow for a millennium, and are sent out again. The matter invested by
these forms is drawn from 'an huge eternall *Chaos*,' which
is the *prima materia;* this is 'eterne,' but the forms are

variable, and decay. Time rules over them, which is represented as disastrous; and it is disastrous that sexual bliss
is not immortal, only the agent of a limited immortality,
athanasia.

Robert Ellrodt, who has written the best study of the
Garden, has no trouble in showing that the form-matter-
substance relation in the poem is medieval commonplace;
it is, if one word must do the work, Augustinian. The
Garden is a symbol of the total act of creation: the seeds
pre-exist, continuous reunion of forms with indestrucible
matter fills the world with generated life. The topics are,
in another language, the eternal material substrate, the
forms or *rationes* (distinguished, as Ellrodt fails to indicate,
from the forms of the *nous* in the allegory of the descent
of Venus). There are some difficulties, admittedly, which
I here ignore, in the way of full allegorical interpretation;
but broadly speaking Spenser is talking about the quasi-
immortality of the generative cycle.

When we come to the allegory of Venus and Adonis the
going is harder. Ellrodt thinks that the form-substance-
matter section is now over, and that Adonis is the sun, as
mythographers often said, the boar being winter; though
wounded by the boar, Adonis is 'by succession made per-
petuall' and revives in the spring. This, I think, misses the
main point. Spenser has been talking about a quasi-eter-
nity and so about an order of duration neither temporal
nor eternal. It is untrue that the sun, like Adonis, is 'hid
from the world, and from the skill of *Stygian* Gods,' and it
is untrue of the sun that Venus, in this seclusion, 'posses-
seth him.' Of what can it be said that it does not 'For ever
die, and ever buried bee / In balefull night, where all

things are forgot,' and that it is, although 'subject to mortalitie,' nevertheless 'eterne in mutabilitie'—

> And by succesion made perpetuall,
> Transformed oft, and chaunged diverslie—

and what may be called 'the Father of all formes'? Not the sun, certainly. But of the generative cycle it can be said; by the power and consent of Venus it achieves its own kind of eternity, perpetual though changing. Adonis isn't matter, an impossible reading though it has been proposed, and he is not the sun. He is the entire biological cycle, conceived as subsisting in the *aevum*. This is what defeats the boar, for the boar is death, the power which, in a fallen world, seeks to make all kinds, in Milton's word, 'unimmortal.'

We can say, then, that Spenser's Garden takes account of the fiction designed to reconcile the evidence for an eternal world with the denial of such a world in Christianity. Spenser, as I've said, was deeply interested in precisely such fictions, and in the situations which produced them: love, for example, and empire, mutability and constancy. His editor called the Seventh Book, of which only the Mutability Cantos survive, the Legend of Constancy; and in it Spenser directly confronts mutability not only with the *nunc stans,* the constancy of eternity, but with such perpetuity, such immutability, as may be predicated of the *nunc movens.* Mutability is in part an essential aspect of the creation, in part a consequence of the Fall. The variety and beauty of the world are, in ordinary experience, inextricably associated with mutability; and the Cantos are accordingly a celebration of the diverse creation. The reply to Mutability comes from Natura, not from the

God of the great Sabbath; her approach is signalled in a
stanza of sexual mystery (like the Phoenix and the Venus
of Book IV, who are also inhabitants of the *aevum,* she is
represented as hermaphrodite) and flowers spring up at
her approach. She is the goddess of what lives and changes
in time under the conditions of a kind of immortality
which is by definition of time. Her judgment begins with
an admission that the nature of created things is to change;
but whereas Mutability stresses the decay inherent in this
process—as in vii.18—Nature explains that change is here
an agent of permanence:

> being rightly wayd
> They are not changed from their first estate;
> But by their change their being doe dilate:
> And turning to themselves at length againe,
> Doe worke their owne perfection so by fate:
> Then over them Change doth not rule and raigne:
> But they raigne over change, and doe their states maintaine.

In the generative cycle, created things affirm their own
kind of eternity by the perpetuation of species in change.
Nature adds, in the last stanza of the Canto, that if Mutability's desires were realized and the world reduced to
merely errant matter without the permanence of specific
forms, the world would be at an end, and so would her
power in it, for at that time all change would cease. The
perpetuities of the *aevum* are proper only to a universe
in which there is time; when that universe is reduced to its
first nothing, and there is only the *nunc stans,* the human
use of *aevum* ends. The vision of eternal constancy follows
at once, in the last stanzas of the poem, the fragmentary
Eighth Canto.

The discords of our experience—delight in change, fear of change; the death of the individual and the survival of the species, the pains and pleasures of love, the knowledge of light and dark, the extinction and the perpetuity of empires—these were Spenser's subject; and they could not be treated without this third thing, a kind of time between time and eternity. He does not make it easy to extract philosophical notions from his text; but that he is concerned with the time-defeating *aevum*, and uses it as a concord-fiction, I have no doubt. 'The seeds of knowledge,' as Descartes observed, 'are within us like fire in flint; philosophers educe them by reason, but the poets strike them forth by imagination, and they shine the more clearly.' We leave behind the philosophical statements, with their pursuit of logical consequences and distinctions, for a free, self-delighting inventiveness, a new imagining of the problems. Spenser used something like the Augustinian seminal reasons; he was probably not concerned about later arguments against them, finer discriminations. He does not tackle the questions, in the Garden cantos, of concreation, but carelessly—from a philosophical point of view—gives matter chronological priority. The point that creation necessitates mutability he may have found in Augustine, or merely noticed for himself, without wondering how it could be both that and a consequence of the Fall; it was an essential feature of one's experience of the world, and so were all the arguments, precise or not, about it.

Now one of the differences between doing philosophy and writing poetry is that in the former activity you defeat your object if you imitate the confusion inherent in an unsystematic view of your subject, whereas in the second you must in some measure imitate what is extreme and

scattering bright, or else lose touch with that feeling of
bright confusion. Thus the schoolmen struggled, when
they discussed God, for a pure idea of simplicity, which
became for them a very complex but still rational issue:
for example, an angel is less simple than God but simpler
than man, because a species is less simple than pure being
but simpler than an individual. But when a poet discusses
such matters, as in say 'Air and Angels,' he is making some
human point, in fact he is making something which is,
rather than discusses, an angel—something simple that
grows subtle in the hands of commentators. This is why
we cannot say the Garden of Adonis is wrong as the Faculty
of Paris could say the Averroists were wrong. And Donne's
conclusion is more a joke about women than a truth about
angels. Spenser, though his understanding of the expression
was doubtless inferior to that of St. Thomas, made in the
Garden stanzas something 'more simple' than any section
of the *Summa*. It was also more sensuous and more passionate. Milton used the word in his formula as Aquinas used
it of angels; poetry is more simple, and accordingly more
difficult to talk about, even though there are in poetry
ideas which may be labelled 'philosophical.'

All the same, poets think, and are of their time; so that
poets of Spenser's time, though they might feel as Bacon
did about the 'vermicular questions' of the schoolmen,
owed much to their conquests. As De Wulf observed, the
scholastic synthesis is too faithful a reflection of the Western mind for complete abandonment—it 'remained in all
men a fixed point of reference for their sensibilities.' And
the change they made in the human way of feeling time
affected not only philosophical poetry like Spenser's. Stevens admired, and for good reason, a remark of Jean Paul-

han's, that the poet 'creates confidence in the world,'—'la confiance que le poète fait naturellement—et nous invite à faire—au monde.' But he added that this is not in itself one of the differentiae between poets and philosophers, because in a different way philosophers also are concerned in the creation of this confidence, in the humanizing of the world by such fictions as causality, or angels. And if times changed as they did, we should expect to find this in the greatest creator of confidence, Shakespeare.

The subject being so enormous, I ask you to consider only one or two brief points. I said in an earlier talk that tragedy may be thought of as the successor of apocalypse, and this is evidently in accord with the notion of an endless world. In *King Lear* everything tends toward a conclusion that does not occur; even personal death, for Lear, is terribly delayed. Beyond the apparent worst there is a worse suffering, and when the end comes it is not only more appalling than anybody expected, but a mere image of that horror, not the thing itself. The end is now a matter of immanence; tragedy assumes the figurations of apocalypse, of death and judgment, heaven and hell; but the world goes forward in the hands of exhausted survivors. Edgar haplessly assumes the dignity; only the king's natural body is at rest. This is the tragedy of sempiternity; apocalypse is translated out of time into the *aevum*. The world may, as Gloucester supposes, exhibit all the symptoms of decay and change, all the terrors of an approaching end, but when the end comes it is not an end, and both suffering and the need for patience are perpetual. We discover a new aspect of our quasi-immortality; without the notion of *aevum*, and the doctrine of kingship as a duality, existing in it and in time, such tragedy would not be possible.

What temporal image of the world do we derive from *Macbeth?* It is, to use the word the play forces on us, equivocal. The play, uniquely concerned with prophecy, begins with a question about the future: 'When shall we three meet again?' The speaker adds, without much apparent sense: 'In thunder, lightning, or in rain?' But these are three conditions which flourish, so to say, in the same hedgerow; they do not differ so completely as to be presentable as mutually exclusive alternatives. For a demon who can see into the cause of things a forecast of bad weather in Scotland is no great enterprise, and the either-ors of the question merely include, in an ironical way, a pointless selection of some aspects of futurity at the expense of others. The answer to the question is:

> When the hurlyburly's done,
> When the battle's lost and won.

Hurlies are to burlies as thunder to lightning, and lost battles are normally also won. The future is split by man-made antitheses, absurdly doubled or trebled in a parody of the uncertainties of human prediction. 'Fair is foul and foul is fair'; it depends upon the nature of the observer's attention, or on the estimate he makes of his own interest.

This is what L. C. Knights called 'metaphysical pitch and toss,' a good phrase, because pitch is to toss as hurly is to burly. It is also a parody of prophetic equivocation, a device as ancient as the Delphic oracle. All plots have something in common with prophecy, for they must appear to educe from the prime matter of the situation the forms of a future. The best of them, thought Aristotle, include

a *peripeteia* no less dependent than the other parts upon
'our rule of probability or necessity' but arising from that
in the original situation to which we have given less attention; *peripeteia* is equivocating plot, and it has been compared, with some justice, to irony. Now *Macbeth* is above
all others a play of prophecy; it not only enacts prophecies, it is obsessed by them. It is concerned with the desire
to feel the future in the instant, to be transported beyond
the ignorant present. It is about failures to attend to the
part of equivoque which lacks immediate interest (as if
one should attend to hurly and not to burly). It is concerned, too, with the equivocations inherent in language.
Hebrew could manage with one word for 'I am' and 'I shall
be'; Macbeth is a man of a different temporal order. The
world feeds his fictions of the future. When he asks the
sisters 'what are you?' their answer is to tell him what he
will be.

   Macbeth, more than any other of Shakespeare's plays, is
a play of crisis, and its opening is a figure for the seemingly
atemporal agony of a moment when times cross; when our
usual apprehension of successive past and future is translated into another order of time. Perhaps one can convey
this best by a glance at an earlier and prototypical chooser,
St. Augustine. He wrote about this moment, when one is
confronted by the lost and won of the future; a moment
when the gap between desire and act is wide. Though
certain of the end desired, he was 'at strife' with himself;
the choices to be made were 'all meeting together in the
same juncture of time.' He said within himself, 'Be it done
now, be it done now'; but he still hesitated between fair
and foul, and cried, 'How long? How long? Tomorrow and
tomorrow?' This is the time when the soul distends itself

to include past and future; and the similarities of language and feeling remind us that Macbeth had also to examine the relation between what may be willed and what is predicted. Throughout the early scenes we are being prepared by triple questions and double answers for the soliloquy at the end of the first Act, which is the speech of a man at this same juncture of time. The equivocating witches conflate past, present, and future; Glamis, Cawdor, Scotland. They are themselves, like the future, fantasies capable of objective shape. Fair and foul, they say; lost and won; lesser and greater, less happy and much happier. They dress the present in the borrowed robes of the future, in the equivoques of prophecy. The prophecies, as Macbeth notes, are in themselves neither good nor ill; but they bring him images of horror that swamp the present, so that 'nothing is / But what is not.' They bring him to that juncture of time so sharply defined by Brutus—the time 'Between the acting of a dreadful thing / And the first motion'—as being like a hideous dream. It is an interim in which the patient is denied the relief of time's successiveness; it seems never to end. His life is balanced on the point of nightmare, and so is time. Hence the see-saw language: *highly–holily, fair–foul, good–ill.*

The great soliloquy begins by wishing away the perpetuity of this moment. It is curious that we should have made a proverb of the expression 'be-all and end-all.' It was not proverbial for Shakespeare—he invented it; it grows out of the theme and language of the play. To be and to end are, in time, antithetical; their identity belongs to eternity, the *nunc stans.* In another way, the phrase is a pregnant conflation of crisis and an end immanent in it. Macbeth would select one aspect of the equivocal future

and make it a perpetual present, and Shakespeare gives
him the right crisis-word, the see-saw of be-all and end-all.
He did use a proverb in the speech, at its very outset; you
will find the source of 'If it were done when 'tis done' in
Tilley ('the thing that is done is not to do') if you are sure
that Shakespeare is not remembering Augustine (or Jesus:
'That thou doest do quickly' John xiii.27).

Macbeth is saying that if an act could be without succession, without temporal consequence, one would welcome it out of a possible future into actuality; it would be
like having *hurly* without *burly*. But acts without 'success'
are a property of the *aevum*. Nothing in time can, in that
sense be *done*, freed of consequence or equivocal aspects.
Prophecy by its very forms admits this, and so do plots. It
is a truism confirmed later by Lady Macbeth: 'What's
done cannot be undone.' The act is not an end. Macbeth,
in the rapt, triple manner of the play, three times wishes
it were: if the doing were an end, he says; if surcease can-
celled success, if 'be' were 'end.' But only the angels make
their choices in non-successive time, and 'be' and 'end' are
one only in God. Macbeth moves to abandon the project.
He is dissuaded by his wife in a speech which brings past,
present, and future tenses to bear at one juncture: '*Was*
the hope drunk...?...*Art* thou afeard / To be the same
in...act...as...in desire?...*Will* you let "I dare not"
wait upon "I would"...?' She seeks the abolition of the
interim between desire and act, the shrinking allowance
of time in which men are permitted to consider their desires in terms of God's time as well as their own.

The distinction is ancient. Christ waited for his *kairos*,
refusing to anticipate the will of his Father; that is what
he meant when he said 'Tempt not the Lord thy God.' So

Irenaeus explains; and when we sin we act against God's
time and 'arrogate to ourselves a sort of eternity, to "take
the long view" and "make sure of things," ' as Clement
observed. Hence, according to Hans Urs von Balthasar,
'the restoration of order by the Son of God had to be the
annulment of that premature snatching at knowledge . . .
the repentant return from a false, swift transfer into eternity to a true, slow confinement in time.' The choice is
between time and eternity. There is, in life, no such third
order as that Macbeth wishes for. In snatching at a future
he has to take *hurly* with *burly*.

The whole of *Macbeth* is penetrated by the language of
times, seasons, prophecies; after the interim, the acting of
the dreadful thing brings Macbeth under the rule of time
again, it anticipates his dread exploits, mangles him to the
point where he can no longer even pretend to understand
its movement. Of Time's revenges, of the great temporal
equivocations in this play I cannot now speak. But it is
true that the crisis of Macbeth's choice, as surely as the
dead King, is 'the great Doom's image'; that the choice of
angelic or divine time was his presumption, and that he
accordingly suffers in time, having chosen his end at the
moment of crisis. To await the season, as Jesus did ('the
time prefixed I waited,' as he says in Milton) or as Gloucester must learn to do in *Lear*, and as Hamlet also learns,
is another solution than Macbeth's.

For *Hamlet* is another play of protracted crisis, and I
think one could show there also the deliberate clash of
chronos and *kairos*, the obsessive collocation of past, present, and future at a moment that seems to require action
the outcome of which can only be ambiguously predicted.
Finally it is known that the readiness is all; that our

choices have their season, which is another time from that in which we feel we live, though, like the time of angels, it intersects our time. The *kairos* arrives, the moment when at last the time is free, by means of a divine *peripeteia*, by accidental judgments and purposes mistook; we cannot make ready for it simply by 'taking the long view.' And when it comes it is an end, in so far as human affairs have ends. It is not a universal end, merely an image of it. In the central tragedy, *Lear*, universality is explicitly disavowed; we have an image of an end, but the dignity survives into a kind of eternity, an *aevum*. This has no necessary implications of happiness; not only Malcolm but Edgar, as princes, and not only princes but the damned in hell, inhabit the *aevum*.

What, then, can Shakespearean tragedy, on this brief view, tell us about human time in an eternal world? It offers imagery of crisis, of futures equivocally offered, by prediction and by action, as actualities; as a confrontation of human time with other orders, and the disastrous attempt to impose limited designs upon the time of the world. What emerges from *Hamlet* is—after much futile, illusory action—the need of patience and readiness. The 'bloody period' of *Othello* is the end of a life ruined by unseasonable curiosity. The millennial ending of *Macbeth*, the broken apocalypse of *Lear*, are false endings, human periods in an eternal world. They are researches into death in an age too late for apocalypse, too critical for prophecy; an age more aware that its fictions are themselves models of the human design on the world. But it was still an age which felt the human need for ends consonant with the past, the kind of end Othello tries to achieve by his final speech; complete, concordant. As usual, Shakespeare allows him his *tock;* but he will not pretend that the clock does not go forward. The human perpetuity which Spenser set against our imagery of the end is represented here also by the kingly announcements of Malcolm, the election of Fortinbras, the bleak resolution of Edgar.

In apocalypse there are two orders of time, and the earthly runs to a stop; the cry of woe to the inhabitants of the earth means the end of their time; henceforth 'time shall be no more.' In tragedy the cry of woe does not end succession; the great crises and ends of human life do not stop time. And if we want them to serve our needs as we stand in the middest we must give them patterns, understood relations as Macbeth calls them, that defy time. The concords of past, present, and future towards which the soul extends itself are out of time, and belong to the duration which was invented for angels when it seemed difficult to deny that the world in which men suffer their ends is dissonant in being eternal. To close that great gap we use fictions of complementarity. They may now be novels or philosophical poems, as they once were tragedies, and before that, angels.

What the gap looked like in more modern times, and how more modern men have closed it, is the preoccupation of the second half of this series.

IV

...after us, the Savage God...

YEATS

The Modern Apocalypse

At this point I want to take up the patterns of apocalypse, as I sketched them in the first talk, and consider their relevance to our own times. It may be recalled that I spoke of certain arbitrarily chosen aspects of apocalyptic thinking and feeling: of the Terrors, of Decadence and Renovation, of Transition, and of Clerkly Scepticism. I shall be referring once more to these. Once again the context in which I shall talk about it is primarily a literary context; one of the purposes of the talk will be to provide hints towards what A. O. Lovejoy might have called 'the discrimination of modernisms.' This is possible, I think, because of the admittedly apocalyptic tenor of much radical thinking about the arts in our century, and because, given this interest common to the modernisms, one may distinguish between them in terms of their different treatments of the paradigm.

It has been my argument that there must be a link between the forms of literature and other ways in which, to quote Erich Auerbach, 'we try to give some kind of order and design to the past, the present and the future.' One of these ways is crisis. I take it that I should begin by saying something about the modern sense of crisis. When you

read, as you must almost every passing day, that <u>ours is</u>
<u>the great age of crisis</u>—technological, military, cultural—
you may well simply nod and proceed calmly to your
business; for this assertion, upon which a multitude of
important books is founded, is nowadays no more surprising than the opinion that the earth is round. <u>There seems</u>
<u>to me to be some danger in this situation, if only because</u>
<u>such a myth, uncritically accepted, tends like prophecy to</u>
<u>shape a future to confirm it.</u> Nevertheless crisis, however
<u>facile the conception, is inescapably a central element in</u>
<u>our endeavours towards making sense of our world.</u>

   <u>It seems to be a condition attaching to the exercise of</u>
<u>thinking about the future that one should assume one's</u>
<u>own time to stand in an extraordinary relation to it. The</u>
<u>time is not free, it is the slave of a mythical end. We think</u>
<u>of our own crisis as pre-eminent, more worrying, more</u>
<u>interesting than other crises.</u> Mr. McLuhan, to take one
instance of importance to students of the arts, places us
at the interesting moment of what he thinks of as a galactic
interpenetration. Auerbach found the driving force for his
powerful synoptic philology in a conviction that his was
the only moment, the moment of unprecedented cultural
crisis, when one could achieve a clear awareness of the true
character of Europe; for 'European civilization is approaching the term of its existence,' is about to be engulfed
in another historical unity. Even the scholar who studies
crisis as a recurrent, if not perpetual, historical phenomenon, tends to single out ours as the major instance. Sorokin, in his *Social Philosophies in an Age of Crisis,* considers other people's crises— 'painful transitional situations' as he calls them—in general, but works throughout
on the assumption that 'the twentieth century is the period

of the greatest crisis . . . a catastrophic transition to a new
culture.' Well may modern philosophies of history, he says,
be eschatological in character.

Now I also believe that there is a powerful eschatological
element in modern thought and that it is reflected in the
arts, as 'Guernica' is said to reflect medieval apocalypses
that interested Picasso; but I don't find it easy to see the
uniqueness of our situation. It is commonplace to talk
about our historical situation as uniquely terrible and in
a way privileged, a cardinal point of time. But can it really
be so? It seems doubtful that our crisis, our relation to
the future and to the past, is one of the important differences between us and our predecessors. Many of them felt
as we do. If the evidence looks good to us, so it did to them.
Perhaps if we have a terrible privilege it is merely that we
are alive and are going to die, all at once or one at a time.
Other people have noticed this, and expressed their feelings about it in images different from ours, armies in the
sky, for example, or a palpable Antichrist; and these we
have discarded. But it would be childish to argue, in a
discussion of how people behave under eschatological
threat, that nuclear bombs are more real and make one
experience more authentic crisis-feelings than armies in
the sky. There is nothing at all distinguishing about eschatological anxiety; it was, one gathers, a feature of Meso-
potamian culture, and it is now a characteristic, often
somewhat reach-me-down in appearance, of what Mr. Lio-
nel Trilling calls the 'adversary culture' or sub-culture in
our society. Of course, since this anxiety attaches itself to
the eschatological means available, it is associated with
changing images. And we can best talk about the differentiae of modern crisis in terms of the literature it pro-

duces; it is by our imagery of past and present and future, rather than from our confidence in the uniqueness of our crisis, that the character of our apocalypse must be known.

I leave aside bogus apocalypse, and also demotic apocalypse, though it still flourishes—and attend to more serious examples of the pattern I mentioned earlier. It is a pattern of anxiety that we shall find recurring, with interesting differences, in different stages of modernism. Its recurrence is a feature of our cultural tradition, if not ultimately of our physiology, for in some measure our ways of thinking and feeling about our position in the middest, and our historical position, always at the end of an epoch, are determined. 'It is a peculiarity of the imagination that it is always at the end of an era.' We make sense of the past as of a book or a psalm we have read or recited, and of the present as a book the seals of which we shall see opened; the only way to do this is to project fears and guesses and inferences from the past onto the future. St. Augustine described the condition in his *Confessions*. The moments we call crises are ends and beginnings. We are ready, therefore, to accept all manner of evidence that ours is a genuine end, a genuine beginning. We accept it, for instance, from the calendar.

Our sense of epoch is gratified above all by the ends of centuries. Sometimes, indeed, it appears that we induce events to occur in accordance with this secular habit of mind. I have spoken briefly of the year 1000 as typical; but I suppose for most of us the best known outbreak of *fin de siècle* phenomena occurred at the end of the nineteenth century; at any rate, it was in that century that the expression became current. Certainly there was a deal of apocalyptic feeling at that time, not least in the revival of imperial mythologies both in England and Germany, in the 'decadence' which became a literary category, and which produced Nordau's book ('it is as though the morrow could not link itself with today. Things as they are totter and plunge'), in the utopian renovationism of some political sects and the anarchism of others. This large and interesting subject we must here forgo, except to maintain that the whole concurrence of *fin de siècle* phenomena amply illustrates Focillon's thesis, that we project our existential anxieties on to history; there is a real correlation between the ends of centuries and the peculiarity of our imagination, that it chooses always to be at the end of an era.

Naturally this fuss about centuries can be seen to be based on the arbitrary calendar; it is known for a myth. You sometimes hear people say, with a certain pride in their clerical resistance to the myth, that the nineteenth century really ended not in 1900 but in 1914. But there are different ways of measuring an epoch. 1914 has obvious qualifications; but if you wanted to defend the neater, more mythical date, you could do very well. In 1900 Nietzsche died; Freud published *The Interpretation of Dreams;* 1900 was the date of Husserl's *Logic,* and of Russell's *Critical Exposition of the Philosophy of Leibniz.* With an exquisite sense of timing Planck published his quantum hypothesis in the very last days of the century, December 1900. Thus, within a few months, were published works which transformed or transvalued spirituality, the relation of language to knowing, and the very locus of human uncertainty, henceforth to be thought of not as an imperfection of the human apparatus but part of the nature of things, a condition of what we may know. 1900, like 1400 and 1600 and 1000, has the look of a year that ends a *saeculum.* The mood of *fin de siècle* is confronted by a harsh historical *finis saeculi.* There is something satisfying about it, some confirmation of the rightness of the patterns we impose. But as Focillon observed, the anxiety reflected by the *fin de siècle* is perpetual, and people don't wait for centuries to end before they express it. Any date can be justified on some calculation or other.

And of course we have it now, the sense of an ending. It has not diminished, and is as endemic to what we call modernism as apocalyptic utopianism is to political revolution. When we live in the mood of end-dominated crisis, certain now-familiar patterns of assumption become evident. Yeats will help me to illustrate them.

For Yeats, an age would end in 1927; the year passed without apocalypse, as end-years do; but this is hardly material. 'When I was writing *A Vision,*' he said, 'I had constantly the word "terror" impressed upon me, and once the old Stoic prophecy of earthquake, fire and flood at the end of an age, but this I did not take literally.' Yeats is certainly an apocalyptic poet, but he does not take it literally, and this, I think, is characteristic of the attitude not only of modern poets but of the modern literary public to the apocalyptic elements. All the same, like us, he believed them in some fashion, and associated apocalypse with war. At the turning point of time he filled his poems with images of decadence, and praised war because he saw in it, ignorantly we may think, the means of renewal. 'The danger is that there will be no war. . . . Love war because of its horror, that belief may be changed, civilization renewed.' He saw his time as a time of transition, the last moment before a new annunciation, a new gyre. There was horror to come: 'thunder of feet, tumult of images.'

But out of a desolate reality would come renewal. In short, we can find in Yeats all the elements of the apocalyptic paradigm that concern us. There are the Terrors; the clerkly scepticism proper to a learned aristocrat confronted by these images of horror; a deep conviction of decadence and a prophetic confidence of renovation; and all this involved in the belief that his moment was the moment of supreme crisis, when one age changed into another by means of a movement he called a 'gradual coming and increase,' an 'antithetical multiform influx.'

We have our Terrors, and specific images of them, though, as I have remarked, these do not distinguish us essentially from other apocalyptists. They function as one might expect in an age of easy communications, under the disadvantage of too easy access; they can be used as a cover for more indulgent aspects of *fin de siècle* conduct. We do not, on the whole, indulge in the number mysticism which usually attended speculation on the Johannine Last Days, though it might be thought that the forty-four steps of escalation—the arithmology of the unthinkable—are a substitute for the seven seals and the blasts on the trumpet. What is certain is that we are interested in decadence and renovation; the basis of this is perhaps primitive, though its expression can be extremely sophisticated. For example, the original Marxist ideology, however tenuously it survives in modern Communism, has not only an inherent utopian element but an element of annunciatory violence. If there is something of this in the modern revolt of the young, as there is also in the revolt of the Negro, we must not expect to limit it to such special groups. In general, we seem to combine a sense of decadence in society—as evidenced by the concept of alienation, which, supported

by a new interest in the early Marx, has never enjoyed
more esteem—with a technological utopianism. In our ways
of thinking about the future there are contradictions
which, if we were willing to consider them openly, might
call for some effort towards complementarity. But they lie,
as a rule, too deep. We continue to assume, as people always have done, that there is a tolerable degree of con-
formity between the disconfirmed apocalypse and a respect-
ably modern view of reality and the powers of the mind.
In short, we retain our fictions of epoch, of decadence and
renovation, and satisfy in various ways our clerkly scepticism about these and similar fictions.

There is one other element of the apocalyptic tradition
to be considered, namely transition. I said a minute ago
that one of the assumptions prevalent in sophisticated
apocalyptism was what Yeats called 'antithetical multiform
influx'—the forms assumed by the inrushing gyre as the
old one reaches its term. The dialectic of Yeats's gyres is
simple enough in essence; they are a figure for the co-existence of the past and future at the time of transition. The
old narrows to its apex, the new broadens towards its base,
and the old and new interpenetrate. Where apex and base
come together you have an age of very rapid transition.
Actually, on Yeats's view of the historical cycle, there were
transient moments of perfection, or what he called Unity
of Being; but there was no way of making these permanent, and his philosophy of history is throughout transitional. In this he is not, of course, original; but his emphasis on the traditional character of our own pre-apocalyptic
moment, in contrast with those exquisite points of time
when life was like the water brimming beautifully but

unstably over the rim of a fountain, seems, for all the privacy of the expression, characteristically modern.

It is commonplace that our times do in fact suffer a more rapid rate of change technologically, and consequently in the increase of social mobility, than any before us. There is nothing fictive about that, and its implications are clear in our own day-to-day lives. What is interesting, though, is the way in which this knowledge is related to apocalypse, so that a mere celebratory figure for social mobility, like *On the Road*, acquires apocalyptic overtones and establishes the language of an elect; and the way in which writers, that is to say, clerks, are willing to go along, arguing that the rate of change implies revolution or schism, and that this is a perpetual requirement; that the stage of transition, like the whole of time in an earlier revolution, has become *endless*.

This is the modern apotheosis of Joachism: the belief that one's own age is transitional between two major periods turns into a belief that the transition itself becomes an age, a *saeculum*. We strip the three-and-a-half years of the Beast, which was the original Johannine period glossed by Joachim, of all its 'primitive' number associations, and are left with eternal transition, perpetual crisis.

Crisis is a way of thinking about one's moment, and not inherent in the moment itself. Transition, like the other apocalyptic phases, is, to repeat Focillon's phrase, an 'intemporal agony'; it is merely that aspect of successiveness to which our attention is given. The fiction of transition is our way of registering the conviction that the end is immanent rather than imminent; it reflects our lack of confidence in ends, our mistrust of the apportioning of history to epochs of this and that. Our own epoch is the epoch of nothing positive, only of transition. Since we move from transition to transition, we may suppose that we exist in no intelligible relation to the past, and no predictable relation to the future. Already those who speak of a clean break with the past, and a new start for the future, seem a little old-fashioned. The spokesman of transitionalism in the arts is Mr. Harold Rosenberg, who expressly announces that the present age of transition is endless; that we have somehow to understand that the criterion by which we decide to receive art into our lives cannot be any criterion deriving from the past, since all such will be inapplicable. The logical development of the doctrine of perpetual transition is that the only criterion by which we may decide if an object has meaning for us is the novelty of the object. This is the situation, and, Mr. Rosenberg believes, it has been thus for some time; he speaks of a 'tradition' of the New. Instead of being a point of balance between two ages, our transition is an age in its own right. The only permanence is in the 'antithetical multiform influx,' which becomes, presumably, 'eterne in mutabilitie.'

Mr. Rosenberg's New is not, in my opinion, a useful criterion; the forms of art—its language—are in their nature a continuous extension or modification of conventions entered into by maker and reader, and this is true even of very original artists so long as they communicate at all. Consequently, novelty in the arts is either communication or noise. If it is noise there is no more to say about it. If it is communication it is inescapably related to something older than itself. 'The innocent eye sees nothing,' the innocent ear hears nothing. This is a brief and perhaps misleading summary of a case that has been argued with great clarity by E. H. Gombrich. I mention it here because it is an indispensable qualification to any argument which assumes that a modernism can be totally schismatic; and because in the immediate context it is relevant to the whole myth of modern transitionalism. For when we speak of transition as permanent we have in a sense reduced the concept to mere noise; it can only be understood by reference to the past. Mr. Rosenberg's New is the Joachite paradigm in the age of the moonshot. It is very sophisticated certainly, but it is a myth. Myths work in the world; and this one has positive implications in the operations of late modernism. It requires to be handled with a high degree of clerical scepticism.

So, indeed, and this is my argument, do all general assumptions concerning crisis and transition. They have a paradigmatic aspect, and can be studied in historical depth. We can think of them as fictions, as useful. If we treat them as something other than they are we are yielding to irrationalism; we are committing an error against which the intellectual history of our century should certainly have warned us. Its ideological expression is fascism; its practical consequence the Final Solution. And we are always in some danger of committing this error. This is the danger I want now to consider in relation to two phases of modernism, our own and that of fifty or so years ago. This is, of course, a crude distinction. What I here, for convenience, call traditionalist modernism has its roots in the period before the Great War, but its flowering came later than that of anti-traditionalist modernism, which was planted by Apollinaire and reaped by Dada. This anti-tradionalist modernism is the parent of our own schismatic modernism; but at both periods the two varieties

here co-existed. Having said this, I shall speak freely of
the traditionalist modernism as the older.

The first phase of modernism, which so far as the English language goes we associate with Pound and Yeats,
Wyndham Lewis and Eliot and Joyce, was clerkly enough,
sceptical in many ways; and yet we can without difficulty
convict most of these authors of dangerous lapses into
mythical thinking. All were men of critical temper, haters
of the decadence of the times and the myths of *mauvaise
foi*. All, in different ways, venerated tradition and had
programmes which were at once modern and anti-schis-
matic. This critical temper was admittedly made to seem
consistent with a strong feeling for renovation; the mood
was eschatological, but scepticism and a refined tradition-
alism held in check what threatened to be a bad case of
literary primitivism. It was elsewhere that the myths ran
riot.

Let us look once more at Yeats. At bottom, he was sceptical about the nonsense with which he satisfied what we
can call his lust for commitment. Now and again he believed some of it, but in so far as his true commitment was
to poetry he recognized his fictions as heuristic and dis-
pensable, 'consciously false.' 'They give me metaphors for
poetry,' he noted. The dolls and the amulets, the swords
and the systems, were the tools of an operationalist. Yeats
was always concerned that what made sense to him in terms
of the system should make sense to others who shared with
him not that arbitrary cipher-system but the traditional
language of poetry. In this way he managed, sometimes
at any rate, to have his cake and to eat it. The rough beast
of the apocalyptic 'Second Coming,' and the spiralling
falcon of the same poem, mean something in the system,

but for the uninstructed reader they continue to mean something in terms of a broader system of cultural and linguistic conventions—the shared information codes upon which literature, like any other method of communication, depends. So too in the later plays, which analytic criticism tells us are very systematic, but which Yeats himself declared must conceal their esoteric substance and sound like old songs. So too with the Byzantium poems, and the Supernatural Songs; even a poem like 'The Statues,' which contains notions that are bound to see inexplicably strange to one who knows nothing of Yeats's historical and art-historical opinions, takes its place in our minds not as a text which codes information more explicitly provided in *On the Boiler* but as one which in some measure our reading of the other poems, and the persona of the wild old man, can justify.

Yeats, in a famous phrase which has occasionally floated free of its context, said that the System enabled him to hold together reality and justice in a single thought. Reality is, in this expression, the sense we have of a world irreducible to human plot and human desire for order; justice is the human order we find or impose upon it. The System is in fact all Justice; in combination with a sense of reality which has nothing whatever to do with it, it became a constituent of poems. The System is a plot, a purely human projection, though not more human than its apparent antithesis, reality, which is a human imagining of the inhuman. For a moment, in that expression, Yeats saw himself as an emperor dispensing equity, transcending both the fact and the pattern; it is what poets do. Only rarely did he forget that whatever devotes itself to justice at the expense of reality, is finally self-destructive.

He might talk about the differences between the symbolic meanings of poetry and those 'emotional restless mimicries of the surface of life' which were for him the characteristics of 'popular realism,' but he understood very well the need for that 'moral element in poetry' which is 'the means whereby' it is 'accepted into the social order and becomes a part of life.' He understands the tension between a paradigmatic order where the price of a formal eternity is inhumanity, and the world of the dying generations; that is the subject of 'Sailing to Byzantium,' the poem I quoted at the outset of these talks. He was talking about this tension again in one of his last poems, when he distinguished between 'Players and painted stage'—the justice of formal poems—and 'the foul rag-and-bone shop of the heart'—the human dirt and disorder that underlie them. The whole history of Yeats's style, which from the earliest times, before the turn of the century, he was trying to move towards colloquial uncertainty, reflects this regard for the reality that will not be reduced. In the end this modernism took on characteristic colours of violence, a sexual toughness and slang to represent what Yeats took to be a modern reality. In his *Oxford Book of Modern Verse* he envied the ease with which other poets were modern, and overvalued them in consequence, perhaps not seeing that they dispensed too readily with justice.

In short, one can say that this poet laboured to speak in terms of a modern reality, to save the phenomena, without forfeiting the use of the paradigm. He did not always succeed; we are surely losing the power to be charmed by the dry paradigmatic rant of such poems as "Under Ben Bulben.' What interests us is, very often, the effort itself. Yeats was deeply committed to his idea of alienation, and his conscious solution of the problems it set was a retreat to myth and to the rituals of the occult; on the one side were the shopkeeping logicians, on the other the seductive and various forms of unreason. What saved him in the end was a confidence basic to the entire European tradition, a confidence in the common language, the vernacular by means of which from day to day we deal with reality as against justice. Everything depends upon a power

> To compound the imagination's Latin with
> The lingua franca et jocundissima.

In the same way, Yeats, though he entertained the fictions of apocalypse, decadence, renovation, transition, saw the need to compound them with the lingua franca of reality. This composition occurs in the poetry. But outside the poetry the situation is different; and here we touch on a general critical failure in early modernism. Yeats wrote a good deal about the Last Days as he saw them, the aristocratic Irish knights who would be faithful and true, the end of a broken-down, odious epoch and the start of another, aristocratic, courtly, eugenic. In poetry this is well enough; it enters the mix of our own minds, which are richer for the new ingredients: 'A Bronze Head' enlarges the imagery by which we represent to ourselves 'This foul world in its decline and fall,' and the terrors are newly lighted by the vision of the daughters of Herodias and that insolent fiend, Robert Artisson. Outside poetry the situation is different. Yeats was enthusiastic for Italian fascism, and supported an Irish fascist movement. The most terrible element in apocalyptic thinking is its certainty that there must be universal bloodshed; Yeats welcomed this with something of the passion that has attended the thinking of more dangerous, because more practical men. 'Send war in our time, O Lord.' Soon the towns lay beaten flat, and the great mass experiment in eugenics began. The dreams of apocalypse, if they usurp waking thought, may be the worst dreams.

At a poet Yeats, at his best, was proof against enchantment by the dream. As a thinker outside poetry he was not; the only reason why this is unimportant is that he had no influence upon those who might have put his beliefs to an operational test. The thoughts of poets may be put to this test. It is true that Yeats's occult speculations are ultimately a mask for a system of aesthetics; nevertheless, as Dewey once observed, 'even aesthetic systems may breed a disposition towards the world and take overt effect.' Yeats is our first example of that correlation between early modernist literature and authoritarian politics which is more often noticed than explained: totalitarian theories of form matched or reflected by totalitarian politics.

Another celebrated example of this correlation is Ezra Pound. I cannot, of course, say much about this complex and bewildering case, but Pound does seem to be an instance of a poet's failure to see that a poetic regress towards paradigms of justice may be carried on without losing touch with the lingua franca, whereas any similar political regress involves immeasurable horror and debasement as well as a loss of reality. To break the set of an inadequate poetic language, to destroy the bonds which tie poetry to a discredited logic, may be tasks calling for new fictions severe and defiant as Pound's pseudo-ideogram. This is a radical reorientation of poetry, an attempt in the Last Days to provide a language of renovation. There is disagreement as to whether this reorientation was well enough executed, sufficiently self-consistent, to achieve what was necessary, the transmission of information by codes only speculatively within access of the reader. But whether the attempt succeeded or not, it could not, in any ordinary sense of the words, be called wrong or dangerous. What is, in this sense, wrong and dangerous is the belief, gratefully learnt by fascism from the innocent pragmatists, that fictions are to be justified or verified by their practical effects. Thus the world is changed to conform with a fiction, as by the murder of Jews. The effect is to insult reality, and to regress to myth. In medieval apocalyptic movements it was usual to identify the Jews as the demonic host of the prophecies (much the same thing had happened earlier in North Africa to the Christians, and can happen to any alien minority of somewhat mysterious habits). The destruction of the demonic host must precede more positive eschatological benefits. A poet's anti-Semitism, a poet's eugenics, may therefore connect him not only with the debased pragmatism of men he ought to despise, but with a crude primitivism of the sort he would never consciously regard as relevant to his own more refined regress. Pound's radio talks were no doubt the work of a man who had lost some of the sense of reality; but above all they represented a failure of what I have called clerical scepticism, and a betrayal rather than a renovation of the tradition which, it is assumed, lies under the threat of destruction by corrupt politics, economics, and language.

Here we find in early modernism a hint of the real treason of the clerks. Its existence is further suggested by Wyndham Lewis. He painted on a theory that the closed society of 'abstraction'—an anti-kinematic, anti-humanist society of rigid hierarchy, ruled by fear—much like the fic-

tion of Worringer, was the best for art. Hence his cult of
deadness, his hatred of all that he called 'Bergsonian,' or
vitalist; of anything that suggested, as relativity theory for
example did, an inalienable degree of independence even
in the minds of the 'peons' or *Untermenschen.* The peons,
according to the heavenly messenger of the apocalyptic
Childermass, are merely 'the multitude of personalities
which God, having created, is unable to destroy.' Sex, time,
liberal thought, are all enemies of paradigmatic rigidity;
and even Pound and Joyce were in their power. Lewis's
own ideas are darkened by smoky polemic and varied by
fits of good nature, but he was certainly anti-feminist,
anti-Semitic, andi-democratic, and had ambivalent views
on colour. T. S. Eliot, in the preface he wrote for a re-issue
of *One-Way Song* in 1955, says that 'the less respectable'
intellectuals 'vociferate the cry of "fascist!"—a term falsely
applied to Lewis, but flung by the *Massenmenschen* at
some, who like Lewis, walk alone.' But this, it must be
said, is characteristic of the evasiveness that until recently
attended discussion of this aspect of modernism; Mr.
Conor Cruise O'Brien has recently castigated it in a study
of Yeats. In 1929 Eliot himself said that Lewis was inclined
'in the direction of some kind of fascism,' and Lewis himself in 1926 said much the same thing. He wrote a book
in praise of Hitler, and found in Nazism a system favour-
able to 'aristocracy of intellect.' He changed these opinions, and in any case it isn't my business to condemn them.
It is sufficient to say that the radical thinking of the early
modernists about the arts implied, in other spheres, opinions of a sort not normally associated with the word
radical.
 It appears, in fact, that modernist radicalism in art—the

breaking down of pseudo-traditions, the making new on a true understanding of the nature of the elements of art— this radicalism involves the creation of fictions which may be dangerous in the dispositions they breed towards the world. There is, for instance, the fantasy of an elect which will end the hegemony of bourgeois or of *Massenmensch*, which will end democracy and all the 'Bergsonian' attitudes to time or human psychology, all the mess which makes up a commonplace modern view of reality. Instead of these there is to be order as the modernist artist understands it: rigid, out of flux, the spatial order of the modern critic or the closed authoritarian society; such a society, we were told in 1940, as would persist, all inferior races, all *Untermenschen*, excluded for a thousand years. All who, in the 'thirties and 'forties, formed their minds on the great moderns but spent their good years opposing fascism, must understand this paradox as in need of resolution. The eschatological fictions of modernism are innocent as ways of reordering the past and present of art, and prescribing for its future:

> Plato thought nature but a spume that plays
> Upon a ghostly paradigm of things.

But to clear that paradigm of natural spume is one thing in poetry or in a theory of poetry; another when the encumbrances can be removed, the spume for ever blown away by a police and a civil service devoted to this final solution.

It is already the fashion to diminish Eliot by calling him derivative, the mouthpiece of Pound, and so forth; and yet if one wanted to understand the apocalypse of early modernism in its true complexity it would be Eliot, I fancy, who would demand one's closest attention. He was

ready to rewrite the history of all that interested him in
order to have past and present conform; he was a poet of
apocalypse, of the last days and the renovation, the destruction of the earthly city as a chastisement of human
presumption, but also of empire. Tradition, a word we
especially associate with this modernist, is for him the
continuity of imperial deposits; hence the importance in
his thought of Virgil and Dante. He saw his age as a long
transition through which the elect must live, redeeming
the time. He had his demonic host, too; the word 'Jew'
remained in lower case through all the editions of the
poems until the last of his lifetime, the seventy-fifth birthday edition of 1963. He had a persistent nostalgia for
closed, immobile hierarchical societies. If tradition is, as
he said in *After Strange Gods*—though the work was sup-
pressed—'the habitual actions, habits and customs' which
represent the kinship 'of the same people living in the
same place' it is clear that Jews do not have it, but also
that practically nobody now does. It is a fiction, a fiction
cousin to a myth which had its effect in more practical
politics. In extenuation it might be said that these writers
felt, as Sartre felt later, that in a choice between Terror
and Slavery one chooses Terror, 'not for its own sake, but
because, in this era of flux, it upholds the exigencies proper
to the aesthetics of Art.'

The fictions of modernist literature were revolutionary,
new, though affirming a relation of complementarity with
the past. These fictions were, I think it is clear, related to
others, which helped to shape the disastrous history of our
time. Fictions, notably the fiction of apocalypse, turn easily
into myths; people will live by that which was designed
only to know by. Lawrence would be the writer to discuss

here, if there were time; apocalypse works in *Woman in Love,* and perhaps even in *Lady Chatterley's Lover,* but not in *Apocalypse,* which is failed myth. It is hard to restore the fictive status of what has become mythical; that, I take it, is what Mr. Saul Bellow is talking about in his assaults on wastelandism, the cant of alienation. In speaking of the great men of early modernism we have to make very subtle distinctions between the work itself, in which the fictions are properly employed, and *obiter dicta* in which they are not, being either myths or dangerous pragmatic assertions. When the fictions are thus transformed there is not only danger but a leak, as it were, of reality; and what we feel about all these men at times is perhaps that they retreated inso some paradigm, into a timeless and unreal vacuum from which all reality had been pumped. Joyce, who was a realist, was admired by Eliot because he modernized myth, and attacked by Lewis because he concerned himself with mess, the disorders of common perception. But *Ulysses* alone of these great works studies and develops the tension between paradigm and reality, asserts the resistance of fact to fiction, human freedom and unpredictability against plot. Joyce chooses a Day; it is a crisis ironically treated. The day is full of randomness. There are coincidences, meetings that have point, and coincidences which do not. We might ask whether one of the merits of the book is not its *lack* of mythologizing; compare Joyce on coincidence with the Jungians and their solemn concord-myth, the Principle of Synchronicity. From Joyce you cannot even extract a myth of Negative Concord; he shows us fiction fitting where it touches. And Joyce, who probably knew more about it than any of the others, was not attracted by the intellectual opportunities or the formal elegance of fascism.

I undertook, at the start of this talk, to attempt something in the line of a discrimination of modernisms. All I shall do is to point out certain differences between this earlier type and some kinds of radical thinking in the arts that go on in our own time. Large and highly relevant areas of information and opinion I shan't be able to refer to at all. The point I'm trying to make is limited, anyway; I hope the partial confrontation of the 'twenties and the 'sixties will make it. After forty years the eschatological pressures have certainly not lessened. Apocalypse is a fashionable word. Transition, decadence-and-renovation, have perhaps become the dominant aspects of apocalypse for the arts, as distinct from politics; and in consequence we have all grown more interested in the possibilities of a break with the past; of considering the present in relation to the end without calculations based on history. The schismatic, to put it another way, has gained in power; early modernism, at any rate the kind I have spoken of, was emphatic about its living relation to the past. Transition is now, as I've said, elevated to secular status. The arts certainly seem to be, in Yeats's words, multiform and antithetical. The succession of styles, as Wyndham Lewis said, may be seen, under one aspect, as a helpless mimicry of the technology. There is no shortage of evidence that this is a difficult state of affairs for critics to work on; the New is not a workable critical concept if you will not give up the hope that there are other indications of value than novelty, and this is only symptomatic of the difficulties experienced by anybody who thinks it wrong to speak of new things in an old language. That the new modernism should be hard to talk about is a sign that there is a gap between the elect and the rest, and that is only another of its apocalyptic aspects. In fact, what distinguishes the new from the older modernism most sharply in this context is not that one is more apocalyptic than the other but that they have such different attitudes to the past. To the older it is a source of order; to the newer it is that which ought to be ignored.

It might be useful here to say a word about Beckett, as a link between the two stages, and as illustrating the shift towards schism. He wrote for *transition*, an apocalyptic magazine (renovation out of decadence, a Joachite indication in the title), and has often shown a flair for apocalyptic variations, the funniest of which is the frustrated millennialism of the Lynch family in *Watt*, and the most telling, perhaps, the conclusion of *Comment c'est*. He is the perverse theologian of a world which has suffered a Fall, experienced an Incarnation which changes all relations of past, present, and future, but which will not be redeemed. Time is an endless transition from one condition of misery to another, 'a passion without form or stations,' to be ended by no *parousia*. It is a world crying out for forms and stations, and for apocalypse; all it gets is vain temporality, mad, multiform antithetical influx.

It would be wrong to think that the negatives of Beckett are a denial of the paradigm in favour of reality in all its poverty. In Proust, whom Beckett so admires, the order, the forms of the passion, all derive from the last book; they are positive. In Beckett, the signs of order and form are more or less continuously presented, but always with a sign of cancellation; they are resources not to be believed in, cheques which will bounce. Order, the Christian paradigm, he suggests, is no longer usable except as an irony; that is why the Rooneys collapse in laughter when they read on the Wayside Pulpit that the Lord will uphold all that fall.

But of course it is this order, however ironized, this continuously transmitted idea of order, that makes Beckett's point, and provides his books with the structural and linguistic features which enable us to make sense of them. In his progress he has presumed upon our familiarity with his habits of language and structure to make the relation between the occulted forms and the narrative surface more and more tenuous; in *Comment c'est* he mimes a virtually schismatic breakdown of this relation, and of his language. It is perfectly possible to reach a point along this line where nothing whatever is communicated, but of course Beckett has not reached it by a long way; and whatever preserves intelligibility is what prevents schism.

This is, I think, a point to be remembered whenever one considers extremely novel, *avant-garde* writing. Schism is meaningless without reference to some prior condition; the absolutely New is simply unintelligible, even as novelty. It may, of course, be asked: unintelligible to whom? —the inference being that a minority public, perhaps very small—members of a circle in a square world—do understand the terms in which the new thing speaks. And certainly the minority public is a recognized feature of modern literature, and certainly conditions are such that there may be many small minorities instead of one large one; and certainly this is in itself schismatic. The history of European literature, from the time the imagination's Latin first made an accommodation with the lingua franca, is in part the history of the education of a public—cultivated but not necessarily learned, as Auerbach says, made up of what he calls *la cour et la ville.* That this public should break up into specialized schools, and their language grow scholastic, would only be surprising if one thought that the existence of excellent mechanical means of communication implied excellent communications, and we know it does not, McLuhan's 'the medium is the message' notwithstanding. But it is still true that novelty of itself implies the existence of what is not novel, a past. The smaller the circle, and the more ambitious its schemes of renovation, the less useful, on the whole, its past will be. And the shorter. I will return to these points in a moment.

A great many different kinds of writing are called *avant-garde*, though the expression itself has virtually dropped out of the vocabulary of writers, who tend or pretend to think that it connotes a past historical period of literature, much as the expression 'modern' has dwindled into a periodic concept. The more *avant-garde* a writer is, the less can he afford to be called *avant-garde*. Nevertheless we all have a vague notion of what it means in terms of current experiment. The work of William Burroughs, for instance, is *avant-garde*. His is the literature of withdrawal, and his interpreters speak of his hatred for life, his junk nihilism, his treatment of the body as a corpse full of cravings. The language of his books is the language of an ending world, its aim, as Ihab Hassan says, is 'self-abolition.' *The Naked Lunch* is a kind of satura, without formal design, unified only by the persistence in its satirical fantasies of outrage and obscenity. Later Burroughs sought a self-abolishing structure, and tried to defeat our codes of continuity, cultural and temporal, by shuffling his prose into random order. 'Writers until the cut-up method was made explicit,'

he says, 'had no way to produce the accident of spontane-
ity.' But it seems that in the logic of the situation we shall
find such accidents happy only when we see in them some
allusion, direct or ironical, to our inherited notions of linguistic and narrative structure; and I am not surprised that
Mr. Hassan, a notable exponent of Burroughs, finds the
method successful only when it is clear that so far from
seeming random the collocations appear to be skilfully
contrived. Hassan's account of Burroughs is thoroughly
apocalyptic, and at all times shows an awareness that this
in itself presupposes a significant past. If Burroughs is a
satirist, and he is, then that also presupposes a past signifi-
cantly altered. And the critic ends with a shrewd word on
the historical associations between utopianism and nihilism: 'to neglect that history,' he says, 'is fateful in this
moment of our crisis.' In a critic so strongly convinced of
the need to adapt criticism to the new demands of a literature proclaiming its total alienation, this seems to me a
very significant remark. It may be that our presuppositions
as to order, in the world and in books, can be radically
changed; Mr. McLuhan is one who would say so. But the
act of writing fictions continues to imply a public of a
certain kind, a public which cannot visualize the conditions which might obtain after its own extinction. Our
experience of the arts suggests that Sartre's little tune in
La Nausée sends a true if tedious message: *Il faut souffrir
en mesure. Mesure* is rhythm, and rhythm implies con-
tinuities and ends and organization.

Somewhere, then, the *avant-garde* language must always
rejoin the vernacular. And randomness, much valued now,
rejoins contrivance. I recently read a poem by Emmett
Williams which was to consist of five thousand lines all

beginning 'The new way . . .'—for instance, 'The new way the jig saws,' or 'The new way the soda pops.' Each of these propositions was to be accompanied by a film projection and a recorded sound, the three randomly mixed. When the poet was required to make a selection of the lines for publication, he made it at random; but he found that the lines chosen had 'acquired unexpectedly, a beginning and an end.' So, he says, 'i destroyed the rest.' (The *i*, it should be noted, is lower-case. This is an index of much triviality in *avant-garde* writing. What is it? A pathetic gesture towards a longed-for illiteracy? If so it is a traditional modernism. A rejection of the upper-case egotism of the *salauds*? It might be worth a thesis.)

Mr. Williams's lines appeared in one of the two rather dismal numbers devoted to the *avant-garde* by the *Times Literary Supplement* a year or so ago. It also contained an essay by Allen Ginsberg which showed rather clearly that for this poet, so much admired by the young and yet in his way so traditionalist a figure, the language appropriate to general descriptions of *avant-gardist* effort is an old-fashioned language: he speaks of the artist's reaction to unbearable modern stimuli, 'the expression in Art of the scream or weep or supplication the EXPRESSION . . . of that infinite Self—which still feels thru the smog of Blakeansatanic war mills, etc.' 'Blakeansatanic' is a non-invention of the same order as lower-case *i*. 'There has been,' Mr. Ginsberg writes, 'an outrage done to my feelings from which I have never recovered.' The emphasis is on a personal pain as original to an act of creation not, at this stage of the argument, discussed. Even in the contributions which emphasized the technical breakthrough, the abolition of the false forms of the past, the new start, the tone

was commonly one of exalted difference, of belonging, in
a phrase I borrowed earlier from a contributor to this
symposium, to a circle in a square world. The technical
talk is a further indication of the fragmentation of the
traditional language of criticism and aesthetics into private
dialects notable rather for a reduction than for an increase
of power and scope. A disregard for the past makes such
movements easy to start; there is an analogy in the history
of heresy, where fanatics often re-invent the doctrines of
earlier sects without knowing it. The *T.L.S.* collection
included an interesting essay by Raoul Haussmann, which
argued that much Neo-Dadaism, as he calls it, is merely
Dadaism with the Art left out. This may seem strangely
put, if you reflect that Tzara called for abolition, spon-
taneity in a tottering world, everybody dancing to 'his
personal boomboom,' freedom, the 'elegant and unpreju-
diced leap.' Haussmann sees that Art, something old, ani-
mated it. The new men have re-invented the Happening,
for example, the Lettrists claim novelty for what was
barely new in 1920; and they do it less well. But schismatic
movements can hardly be expected to care for continuity
and the past; the more schismatic they are, the less they
know about the possibilities of novelty.

The earlier modernists may have picked up something
from Dada before it gave way to the less schismatic sur-
realism; they shared with it a certain anti-intellectualism
and a powerful sense of apocalypse. But they were intellectuals and space-men, not time-men with a special interest in the chaotic moment. On Eliot's view of literature,
for instance, newness is a phenomenon that affects the
whole of the past; nothing on its own can be new. That
alone distinguishes his modernism from avant-gardism.

To return for a moment to the *T.L.S.*, there was one essay which had the clerkly scepticism necessary to observe that what is merely schismatic is likely to be obsolete—to attract the fate it holds to be most shameful. Surprise is the least durable of aesthetic responses; Jonathan Miller, in this paper, argued that we have to learn that early modernism discovered virtually all the possible categories, so that surprise is no longer to be had, except by the abolition of the history of surprises. This does not mean that nothing new can be done; there are rediscoveries, fruitful revaluations, and in the current use of De Sade and Artaud there is an instance of both, a new use for the past. I think Miller's argument is right: that 'the anticipation of the general public is now so comprehensive that even for them the avant-garde seems to have eaten its way out of its own container and dissolved into thin air.' There is an element of convention inescapably present in the work, and also in the associated life-style. There is an element of convention in the dominant mood of crisis and apocalypse. Novelty becomes the inflation of triviality; the apocalypse is signalled by trivial games, mostly not original. Millennial renovationism declines into antithetical multiform influx; there is more noise than information. When the result comes before the clerkly eye of Jonathan Miller, or the disillusioned eye of an old schismatic like Haussmann, it is seen either to conform to existing types, or to sink into non-communicative triviality.

Marx once said that 'the consciousness of the past weighs like a nightmare on the brain of the living,' and it is from that nightmare that the modern apocalyptists want to awake. But the nightmare is part of our condition, part of their material. One generation confronted it in the posture

of the authoritarian traditionalist; another prefers that of
the hipster anarchist. The former, for reasons I tried to
give earlier, was more congenial to the task of making it
new. One could enforce the contrast between them by
comparing typical rhetorics, or attitudes to time and
change. To Lewis the art of the Beats and hipster art would
be Bergsonian. He wrote once of a famous contemporary
novel that it was the 'cheap pastry of stuffy and sadic romance,' a work of 'sweet and viscous sentimentalism.' He
was talking about Proust, not about *An American Dream,*
or *On the Road* (to name one good and one bad book).
Imagine Lewis on the cult of orgasm, or on Allen Ginsberg. The philosopher of the eye would have found hard
words for the philosophers of other organs.

No doubt I have exaggerated the differences between
the two modernisms. There is a continuity between them,
a continuity of crisis; what distinguishes them broadly is
that the older, in an ancient tradition, remade or rewrote
its past, but the latter has a nihilistic, schismatic quality.
It is not unlike the difference between such a church as
the Anglican, professing to sort out traditions, and the
extremist sects, such as Anabaptists. But there were schis-
matics contemporary with early modernism; Lewis already
found them excessive. As I have said, he would surely have
associated some moderns with the time-and-flux men represented by the Bailiff in *The Childermass.* He attacked the
White Negro in advance, and in the figure of Kreisler in
Tarr struck a proleptic blow at the 'melodramatic nihilism' of the later modernists. But there is, I think, between
the two modernisms the broad distinction I have drawn.
Each reacts to a 'painful transitional situation,' but one in
terms of continuity and the other in terms of schism. The

common topics are transition and eschatological anxiety; but one reconstructs, the other abolishes, one decreates and the other destroys the indispensable and relevant past.

To speak clearly on these issues is to attract the charge that one is simply no longer young enough or bright enough to grasp the exciting things that are going on. If what is happening is not a continuation but a mutation, then everything I say is wholly wrong. All these talks may be so much waste paper devoted to the obsolete notion that there is a humanly needed order which we call form; the notion has been attacked at length by the philosophical antiformalist Morse Peckham, for whom art is simply what occurs in a setting and a situation appropriate to a certain kind of attention. But why do we attend? Not because by doing so we can project our own order onto anything, but because some things are designed, in collaboration more or less close between producer and consumer, to accommodate, confirm, and extend that order. There is all the difference here between Schoenberg and random music, between the translogical order of *The Waste Land,* and the random collocations of Emmett Williams, between Ford's cubist novel and the cutup-foldin experiments. However radical the alterations to traditional procedures implied in the first, they are extensions, in a recognizable sense, of a shared language. The others succeed only in so far as they are that, and since they are trying not to be they more often fail.

These distinctions made, it remains to affirm also the continuity of apocalyptic postures. In a world otherwise seen as lacking the form that an end implies, this may seem absurd; indeed it is called so, and highly valued for being so. Apocalypse is a part of the modern Absurd. This is testimony to its vitality, a vitality dependent upon its truth to the set of our fear and desire. Acknowledged, qualified by the scepticism of the clerks, it is—even when ironized, even when denied—an essential element in the arts, a permanent feature of a permanent literature of crisis. If it becomes myth, if its past is forgotten, we sink quickly into myth, into stereotype. We have to employ our knowledge of the fictive. With it we can explain what is essential and eccentric about early modernism, and purge the trivial and stereotyped from the arts of our own time. Great men deceived themselves by neglecting to do this; other men, later, have a programme against doing it. The critics should know their duty.

Part of this duty, certainly, will be to abandon ways of speaking which on the one hand obscure the true nature of our fictions—by confusing them with myths, by rendering spatial what is essentially temporal—and on the other obscure our sense of reality by suggesting that fictions represent some kind of surrender or false consolation. The critical issue, given the perpetual assumption of crisis, is no less than the justification of ideas of order. They have to be justified in terms of what survives, and also in terms of what we can accept as valid in a world different from that out of which they come, resembling the earlier world only in that there is biological and cultural continuity of some kind. Our order, our form, is necessary; our skepticism as to fictions requires that it shall not be spurious. It is an issue central to the understanding of modern literary fiction, and I hope in my next talk to approach it more directly.

V

A dissonance
in the valence of Uranium
led to the discovery

Dissonance
(if you're interested)
leads to discovery

W. C. WILLIAMS, *Paterson* IV

(On the Curies)

Literary Fiction and Reality

TOWARDS the beginning of his novel *The Man Without Qualities*, Robert Musil announces that 'no serious attempt will be made to ... enter into competition with reality.' And yet it is an element in the situation he cannot ignore. How good it would be, he suggests, if one could find in life the simplicity inherent in *narrative order*. 'This is the simple order that consists in being able to say: "When that had happened, then this happened." What puts our mind at rest is the simple sequence, the overwhelming variegation of life now represented in, as a mathematician would say, a unidimensional order.' We like the illusions of this sequence, its acceptable appearance of causality: 'it has the look of necessity.' But the look is illusory; Musil's hero Ulrich has 'lost this elementary narrative element' and so has Musil. *The Man Without Qualities* is multidimensional, fragmentary, without the possibility of a narrative end. Why could he not have his narrative order? Because 'everything has now become non-narrative.' The illusion would be too gross and absurd.

Musil belonged to the great epoch of experiment; after Joyce and Proust, though perhaps a long way after, he is the novelist of early modernism. And as you see he was prepared to spend most of his life struggling with the problems created by the divergence of comfortable story and the non-narrative contingencies of modern reality. Even in the earlier stories he concerned himself with this disagreeable but necessary dissociation; in his big novel he tries to create a new genre in which, by all manner of dazzling devices and metaphors and stratagems, fiction and reality can be brought together again. He fails; but the point is that he had to try, a sceptic to the point of mysticism and caught in a world in which, as one of his early characters notices, no curtain descends to conceal 'the bleak matter-of-factness of things.'

I have spoken in my earlier talks about the operation of clerical scepticism on other kinds of fiction, and you may have felt somewhat sceptical of *my* fictions; but now, when I have to speak of it as a factor in the changing condition of literary fiction, I see that all I shall be doing is to give a large emphasis to what is commonplace. In speaking of a continual attempt on the part of the clerisy to relate, by frequent alteration, an inherited paradigm to a changed sense of reality, we may strain the attention of hearers so long as we speak of physics or law or theology, but as soon as the subject is the novel the argument drops into a perfectly familiar context.

It happens that in our phase of civility, the novel is the central form of literary art. It lends itself to explanations borrowed from any intellectual system of the universe which seems at the time satisfactory. Its history is an attempt to evade the laws of what Scott called 'the land of fiction'—the stereotypes which ignore reality, and whose remoteness from it we identify as absurd. From Cervantes forward it has been, when it has satisfied us, the poetry

which is 'capable,' in the words of Ortega, 'of coping with
present reality.' But it is a 'realistic poetry' and its theme
is, bluntly, 'the collapse of the poetic' because it has to do
with 'the barbarous, brutal, mute, meaningless reality of
things.' It cannot work with the old hero, or with the old
laws of the land of romance; moreover, such new laws and
customs as it creates have themselves to be repeatedly
broken under the demands of a changed and no less brutal
reality. 'Reality has such a violent temper that it does not
tolerate the ideal even when reality itself is idealized.'
Nevertheless, the effort continues to be made. The extrem-
est revolt against the customs or laws of fiction—the anti-
novels of Fielding or Jane Austen or Flaubert or Natalie
Sarraute—creates its new laws, in their turn to be broken.
Even when there is a profession of complete narrative
anarchy, as in some of the works I discussed last week, or
in a poem such as *Paterson*, which rejects as spurious whatever most of us understand as form, it seems that time will
always reveal some congruence with a paradigm—provided
always that there is in the work that necessary element of
the customary which enables it to communicate at all.

I shall not spend much time on matters so familiar to
you. Whether, with Lukács, you think of the novel as
peculiarly the resolution of the problem of the individual
in an open society—or as relating to that problem in respect
of an utterly contingent world; or express this in terms of
the modern French theorists and call its progress a necessary and 'unceasing movement from the known to the
unknown'; or simply see the novel as resembling the other
arts in that it cannot avoid creating new possibilities for
its own future—however you put it, the history of the novel
is the history of forms rejected or modified, by parody,

manifesto, neglect, as absurd. Nowhere else, perhaps, are
we so conscious of the dissidence between inherited forms
and our own reality.

There is at present some good discussion of the issue
not only in French but in English. Here I have in mind
Iris Murdoch, a writer whose persistent and radical thinking about the form has not as yet been fully reflected in
her own fiction. She contrasts what she calls 'crystalline
form' with narrative of the shapeless, quasi-documentary
kind, rejecting the first as uncharacteristic of the novel
because it does not contain free characters, and the second
because it cannot satisfy that need of form which it is easier
to assert than to describe; we are at least sure that it exists,
and that it is not always illicit. Her argument is important
and subtle, and this is not an attempt to restate it; it is
enough to say that Miss Murdoch, as a novelist, finds much
difficulty in resisting what she calls 'the consolations of
form' and in that degree damages the 'opacity,' as she calls
it, of character. A novel has this (and more) in common
with love, that it is, so to speak, delighted with its own
inventions of character, but must respect their uniqueness
and their freedom. It must do so without losing the formal
qualities that make it a novel. But the truly imaginative
novelist has an unshakable 'respect for the contingent';
without it he sinks into fantasy, which is a way of deform-
ing reality. 'Since reality is incomplete, art must not be
too afraid of incompleteness,' says Miss Murdoch. We must
not falsify it with patterns too neat, too inclusive; there
must be dissonance. 'Literature must always represent a
battle between real people and images.' Of course it must
also have form; but as Mrs. Byatt says in her valuable book

on Miss Murdoch, the novelist seems to feel some 'meta-physical regret' about this.

Here, in a subtle philosophical novelist, is what I crudely call the dilemma of fiction and reality. When Miss Murdoch herself succeeds in writing a novel which contains opaque, impenetrable persons in a form which nowhere betrays a collapse from the strict charities of the imagination into the indulgent mythologies of fantasy, we shall have more evidence that the history of the novel is a history of anti-novels.

This, one might add, is likely to be true, even when the good novelist makes no obviously revolutionary proposals. He might even reject the anti-novel as such, and yet possess the power to make constitutional changes so profound that no proclamation of reform could be more effective. There is, for example, Mrs. Spark; her reality is not the brutal chaos of which Ortega speaks, but a radically non-contingent reality to be dealt with in purely novelistic terms, and so related to novels that only a profound virtuosity is needed to make this apparent. In her new novel, which is a work of profound virtuosity, she not only makes these assumptions about the novel, but also considers anti-novels. After all, they exist; and with the panache she reserves for her most deeply serious statements, she includes a sample of one. It is a transcript of a dull day in the Eichmann trial, a day of pure contingency, and yet, under the pressure of the novel's higher reality, it becomes the 'desperate heart' not only of the trial but of the book. The *nouveau roman*, with its deliberately limited, solipsistic realism, is given meaning by inclusion in a higher form. The relation of fiction and reality is uniquely reimagined. And thus the new, even if it restates the old, re-

quires us to undergo the characteristic experience of serious modern fiction, a radical re-appraisal of this relation.
In short, the novelist, though he may aspire—in the language of Tillich—to live in conditions of reality unpro-
tected by myth, has to allow room for different versions of
reality, including what some call mythical and some call
absolute. Also we find that there is an irreducible minimum of geometry—of humanly needed shape or structure
—which finally limits our ability to accept the mimesis of
pure contingency.

But having stressed what Mrs. Spark has in common
with other researchers into novelistic form, one needs also
to point out a deep difference of mood. Those deep and
delightful concordances assume or assert that the world
itself is a land of fiction, a divine fiction which is the supreme fiction because absolutely if strangely true; and that
contingencies, under the pressure of imagination, resolve
themselves into beautiful, arbitrary, and totally satisfying
images of this benign arrangement. Few, I suppose, will
nowadays claim empirical knowledge of such concord. Mrs.
Spark is certainly one who believes that form is a matter
of *recherche,* as the French are always saying; but that
having found it you have a right to be consoled by it, for
the good reason that it is authentic, and reflects, however
imperfectly, a universal plot, an enchanting order of beginning, middle, and end, concords so apt and unexpected
that you laugh or weep when you stumble on them; peripeteias so vast and apparently uncontrolled that nothing
in the literature of comedy or tragedy can do more than
faintly image them. All, rightly seen, is riches, and sin is
behovely; 'all's well that ends well, still the fine's the
crown.' This is not, after all, quite the world of those who

seek 'the courage to be' and to strip reality of the protection of myth. We are all poor; but there is a difference
between what Mrs. Spark intends by speaking of 'slender
means,' and what Stevens called our poverty or Sartre our
need, *besoin*. The poet finds his brief, fortuitous concords,
it is true: not merely 'what will suffice,' but 'the freshness
of transformation,' the 'reality of decreation,' the 'gaiety
of language.' The novelist accepts need, the difficulty of
relating one's fictions to what one knows about the nature
of reality, as his *donnée*.

It is because no one has said more about this situation, or
given such an idea of its complexity, that I want to devote
most of this talk to Sartre and the most relevant of his novels, *La Nausée*. As things go now it isn't of course very
modern; Robbe-Grillet treats it with amused reverence as a
valuable antique. But it will still serve for my purposes.
This book is doubtless very well known to you; I can't un-
dertake to tell you much about it, especially as it has often
been regarded as standing in an unusually close relation
to a body of philosophy which I am incompetent to ex-
pound. Perhaps you will be charitable if I explain that I
shall be using it and other works of Sartre merely as examples. What I have to do is simply to show that *La Nausée* represents, in the work of one extremely important
and representative figure, a kind of crisis in the relation
between fiction and reality, the tension or dissonance between paradigmatic form and contingent reality. That
the mood of Sartre has sometimes been appropriate to
the modern demythologized apocalypse is something I
shall take for granted; his is a philosophy of crisis, but his
world has no beginning and no end. The absurd dishon-
esty of all prefabricated patterns is cardinal to his beliefs;

to cover reality over with eidetic images—illusions persisting from past acts of perception, as some abnormal children 'see' the page or object that is no longer before them
—to do this is to sink into *mauvaise foi*. This expression
covers all comfortable denials of the undeniable—freedom
—by myths of necessity, nature, or things as they are. Are
all the paradigms of fiction eidetic? Is the unavoidable,
insidious, comfortable enemy of all novelists *mauvaise foi?*

Sartre has recently, in his first instalment of autobiography, talked with extraordinary vivacity about the role-
playing of his youth, of the falsities imposed upon him by
the fictive power of words. At the beginning of the Great
War he began a novel about a French private who cap-
tured the Kaiser, defeated him in single combat, and so
ended the war and recovered Alsace. But everything went
wrong. The Kaiser, hissed by the *poilus,* no match for the
superbly fit Private Perrin, spat upon and insulted, became 'somehow heroic.' Worse still, the peace, which
should instantly have followed in the real world if this
fiction had a genuine correspondence with reality, failed
to occur. 'I very nearly renounced literature,' says Sartre.
Roquentin, in a subtler but basically similar situation,
has the same reaction. Later Sartre would find again that
the hero, however assiduously you use the pitchfork, will
recur, and that gaps, less gross perhaps, between fiction
and reality will open in the most close-knit pattern of
words. Again, the young Sartre would sometimes, when
most identified with his friends at the *lycée,* feel himself to
be 'freed at last from the sin of existing'—this is also an
expression of Roquentin's, but Roquentin says it feels like
being a character in a novel.

How can novels, by telling lies, convert existence into

being? We see Roquentin waver between the horror of contingency and the fiction of *aventures*. In *Les Mots* Sartre very engagingly tells us that he *was* Roquentin, certainly, but that he was Sartre also, 'the elect, the chronicler of hells' to whom the whole novel of which he now speaks so derisively was a sort of *aventure*, though what was represented within it was 'the unjustified, brackish existence of my fellow-creatures.' All this is good fun, but it is only another way of talking about a problem which, in a different mood he saw to be serious, namely, the relation between fictions as we use them in our existential crises, and fictions as we construct them in books.

Novels, says Sartre, are not life, but they owe our power upon us, as upon himself as an infant, to the fact that they are somehow like life. In life, he once remarked, 'all ways are barred and nevertheless we must act. So we try to change the world; that is, to live *as if* the relations between things and their potentialities were governed not by deterministic processes but by magic.' The *as if* of the novel consists in a similar negation of determinism, the establishment of an accepted freedom by magic. We make up *aventures*, invent and ascribe the significance of temporal concords to those 'privileged moments' to which we alone award their prestige, make our own human clocks tick in a clockless world. And we take a man who is by definition *de trop*, and create a context in which he isn't.

The novel is a lie only as our quotidian inventions are lies. The power which goes to its making—the imagination —is a function of man's inescapable freedom. This freedom, in Mary Warnock's words, 'expresses itself in his ability to see things which are *not*.' It is by his fiction that we know he is free. It is not surprising that Sartre as ontologist, having to describe many kinds of fictive behaviour, invents stories to do so, thus moving into a middle ground between life and novel. The stories in *L'Etre et le néant* of the girl with her seducer, the waiter who plays the role of waiter, are inventions exemplary of *mauvaise foi;* only in their being related by an explicit philosophical argument, and in their not being related by anything that could be called a plot, do they differ from the story of the lighthouse, or of the sick café proprietor, in *La Nausée.* But of course this single difference is a very great one, and we need to be as clear as possible about it. In a word, it is literary form, something quite different from the form of philosophical discourse. For example, Sartre admired *L'Etranger* because it did not contain a single superfluous episode or image; suppose your novel is about a man as necessarily *de trop,* it must make him and itself the very reverse of that.

This is one reason why *La Nausée* is so challenging. One of the criteria in which we habitually judge novels is that by which Sartre judged Camus's book—by its transfiguration, as it were, of the contingent. But Sartre's novel needs to give very full representation to the horror of contingency; to say, in Miss Murdoch's word, that Sartre 'respects' it gives a very pale notion of the role of contingency as antagonist in *La Nausée.* And deep in the imagery of the book there is a radical representation of this war between what is *de trop* and what must not be *de trop.* Contingency is nauseous and viscous; it has been suggested that the figure is ultimately sexual. This is unformed matter, *materia, matrix;* Roquentin's is ultimately the form-giving male role. He experiences reality in all its contingency, without benefit of human fiction; he resolves to make a fiction. Between his experience and his fiction lies Sartre's book. In so far as it gives structure and form to the metaphysical beliefs expressed in the treatise, it both represents and belies them. Sartre noted of Maurice Blanchot's work that a metaphysic looks different in and out of the water of a novel, and in his own case he cannot avoid this; the novel itself has a hand in the game, and may insist on meanings and relations which the treatise denies or confutes. This is what form does; somewhere along the line it will join what Sartre calls 'bad faith.' There may be an irony in Roquentin's decision to attempt a novel 'beautiful and hard as steel' but is a way of talking about Sartre's own attempt to include contingency in a form which is, in so far as it succeeds, the destroyer of contingency. The novel has, for all that may be said in theory against such a possibility, 'a priori limitations.'

That this is so, and that Sartre's novel demonstrates it, we can see by looking at some of the doctrine that seems in some degree falsified by its appearance in novel form. Take, for example, Sartre's pronouncements on the past —how would they show in a novel? Existentialist man, who has total responsibility for his actions, has no relevant past. He is in a world which he not only never made, but which was never made at all. His world is a chaos without potentiality, and he himself is purely potential nothingness; in the world 'all is act'; potentiality is purely human. To see the thing *pour soi*, as Roquentin does in the park, is to be nauseously aware that 'all is fullness': *mes yeux ne rencontraient jamais que du plein.* When the tree shuddered in the wind, the shudder was not 'a passing from potency to act; it was a thing.' But the world a novel makes (and *La Nausée* makes) is unlike the world of our common experience because it is created and because it has the potency of a humanly imaginative creation. For Aristotle the literary plot was analogous to the plot of the world in that both were eductions from the potency of matter. Sartre denies this for the world, and specifically denies, in the passage just referred to, that without potentiality there is no change. He reverts to the Megaric view of the matter, which Aristotle took such trouble to correct. But this is not our affair. The fact is that even if you believe in a Megaric world there is no such thing as a Megaric novel; not even *Paterson*. Change without potentiality in a novel is impossible, quite simply; though it is the hopeless aim of the cut-out writers, and the card-shuffle writers. A novel which really implemented this policy would properly be a chaos. No novel can avoid being in some sense what Aristotle calls 'a completed action.' This being so, all novels imitate a world of potentiality, even if this implies a philosophy disclaimed by their authors. They have a fixation on the eidetic imagery of beginning, middle, and end, potency and cause.

Novels, then, have beginnings, ends, and potentiality, even if the world has not. In the same way it can be said that whereas there may be, in the world, no such thing as character, since a man is what he does and chooses freely what he does—and in so far as he claims that his acts are determined by psychological or other predisposition he is a fraud, *lâche,* or *salaud*—in the novel there can be no just representation of this, for if the man were entirely free he might simply walk out of the story, and if he had no character we should not recognize him. This is true in spite of the claims of the doctrinaire *nouveau roman* school to have abolished character. And Sartre himself has a powerful commitment to it, though he could not accept the Aristotelian position that it is through character that plot is actualized. In short, novels have characters, even if the world has not.

What about time? It is, effectively, a human creation, according to Sartre, and he likes novels because they concern themselves only with human time, a faring forward irreversibly into a virgin future from ecstasy to ecstasy, in his word, from *kairos* to *kairos* in mine. The future is a fluid medium in which I try to actualize my potency, though the end is unattainable; the present is simply the *pour-soi*, 'human consciousness in its flight out of the past into the future.' The past is bundled into the *en-soi*, and has no relevance. 'What I was is not the foundation of what I am, any more than what I am is the foundation of what I shall be.' Now this is not novel-time. The faring forward is all right, and fits the old desire to know what happens next; but the denial of all causal relation between disparate *kairoi*, which is after all basic to Sartre's treatment of time, makes form impossible, and it would never occur to us that a book written to such a recipe, a set of discontinuous epiphanies, should be called a novel. Perhaps we could not even read it thus: the making of a novel is partly the achievement of readers as well as writers, and readers would constantly attempt to supply the very connections that the writer's programme suppresses. In all these ways, then, the novel falsifies the philosophy.

In Simone de Beauvoir's autobiography there is an account of her telling Ramon Fernandez and Adamov about the novel she is working on, *L'Invitée*. She claims that it is 'a real novel, with a beginning, a middle, and an end.' And real novels do have these. A truly Sartrean novel would be nothing but a discontinuous unorganized middle. And it would be entirely undetermined. But in practice it cannot be so. 'I provided Marcel with a wife,' says Mlle de Beauvoir, 'whom I used as a foil.' Similarly Sartre, in his trilogy *(Les Chemins de la liberté)*, determines many things, for instance, that Lola shall possess the money Matthieu needs for Marcelle's abortion. Here is a piece of virtually nineteenth-century plotting. There is nothing quite so crude in *La Nausée,* but it has its necessary share of contrivance or 'faking.'

The novel, then, provides a reduction of the world different from that of the treatise. It has to lie. Words, thoughts, patterns of word and thought, are enemies of truth, if you identify that with what may be had by phenomenological reductions. Sartre was always, as he explains in his autobiography, aware of their being at variance with reality. One remembers the comic account of this antipathy in Iris Murdoch's *Under the Net,* one of the few truly philosophical novels in English; truth would be found only in a silent poem or a silent novel. As soon as it speaks, begins to be a novel, it imposes causality and concordance, development, character, a past which matters and a future within certain broad limits determined by the project of the author rather than that of the characters. They have their choices, but the novel has its end.*

* There is a remarkable passage in Ortega y Gasset's London essay 'History as a System' (in *Philosophy and History,* ed. Klibansky and Paton, 1936) which very clearly states the issues more notoriously formulated by Sartre. Ortega is discussing man's duty to make himself. 'I invent projects of being and doing in the light of circumstance. This alone I come upon, this alone is given me: circumstance. It is too often forgotten that man is impossible without imagination, without the capacity to invent for himself a conception of life, to "ideate" the character he is going to be. Whether he be original or a plagiarist, man is the novelist of himself . . . Among . . .

It sounds good to say that the novelist is free; that, like the young man who asked Sartre whether he should join the Resistance or stay with his mother, he can be told 'You are free, therefore choose; that is to say, invent.' We may even agree that until he has chosen he will not know the reasons for his choice. But there is in practice this difference between the novelist and the young man as Sartre sees him: the young man will always be free in just this degree; whether he stays with his mother or not, his decision will not be relevant to his next decision. But the novelist is not like that; he is more Thomist than Sartrean, and every choice will limit the next. He has to collaborate with his novel; he grows in bad faith. He is a world in which past, present, and future are related inextricably.

That Sartre is not unaware of this difficulty we can, I think, gather from some of the things he has said about novels. The attack on Mauriac, and on the novels of the past, is founded upon a conviction that they are dishonestly determinate. The characters in a Christian novel, he says, ought surely to be 'centres of indeterminacy' and not the slaves of some fake omniscience. It is by the negation of such formalism that we may make literature a liberating force. 'There is nothing else to spiritualize, nothing else to renew, but this multi-coloured and concrete world with

---

possibilities I must choose. Hence, I am free. But, be it well understood, I am free *by compulsion*, whether I wish to be or not ... To be free means to be lacking in constitutive identity, not to have subscribed to a determined being, to be able to be other than what one was ...' This 'constitutive instability' is the human property lacking in the novels condemned by Sartre and Murdoch. Ortega differs from Sartre on the use of the past; but when he says that his free man is, willy-nilly, 'a second-hand God,' creating his own entity, he is very close to Sartre, who says that to be is to be like the hero in a novel. In one instance the eidetic image is of God, in the other of the Hero.

its weight, its opacity, its zones of generalization, and its swarms of anecdotes.' A novel which tackles these qualities will have no eidetic form, no concordance suggesting false absolutes. Those that have, Mauriac's, for instance, are manipulated, belong to an obsolete world-style, replace reality by myth. But when Sartre comes upon *L'Etranger*, its discontinuous present 'eliminating all the significant links which are also part of the experience,' he says that it is not a novel because, among other things, it lacks 'development'; though he admires it for its economy of organization. Yet 'development' surely implies continuity and a mimesis of the actualization of potency; and organization is form. He has later attacked the *nouveau roman*, which offers, one would have thought, a view of reality congenial to him, on the ground that it is formalistic. It is very difficult to sort this out, but it seems clear enough that what is not taken into account is the novel itself, the collaborator from which neither writer nor reader can free himself, the source of all the falsifying eidetic images.

Let me give one more example of the pressure of these eidetic images, by saying a word about the hero. Robbe-Grillet complains that Sartre failed to do what he intended in *La Nausée:* he names but does not characterize contingency, and is classically connected and chronological; and he lets Roquentin become a kind of hero. Now the images of tragedy and the hero surely do brood over existentialist thought in general; it has been said that the existentialist choice is an adaptation of Christian eschatology, and we should add to that category the eschatological type of the hero. This is why Kott can speak of transferring tragedy and its heroes into the mode of absurdity; accepting his anguish in freedom, the existentialist man repeats the gestures of the tragic hero in a context which is not tragic but absurd. In the novel of Camus, for example, Meursault—the man who 'without any heroics, accepts to die for the truth' as the author puts it—is a gratuitous murderer and not a gratuitous victim; but in many ways he is clearly and literally an Antichrist, with the tradition of Christian heroism rendered absurd in him; we might say the careful meaninglessness of his life is exactly antithetical to the fullness of the concordances found in the life of Jesus. Sartre gives to his anti-hero, in the anguish of freedom, a burden of responsibility which looks absurd in the monstrous world of contingency, but is precisely the burden that we recognize in other literature as tragic: 'when a man commits himself to anything, fully realizing that he is not only choosing what he will be, but is thereby at the same time a legislator deciding for the whole of mankind—in such a moment he cannot escape from the sense of profound and complete responsibility.' This is the hero in a world where existence precedes essence, and where, 'in the present, one is forsaken.' And as Sartre himself clearly sees, to think of a man thus is to think of him as the hero of a novel. If you put such a man in a novel he will in some irreducible measure be shadowed by the eidetic image of the Hero. Like the Kaiser, beaten up by the superbly fit Private Perrin, he becomes *somehow* heroic.

I hope I have now made it clear why I thought it best, in speaking of the dissonances between fiction and reality in our own time, to concentrate on Sartre. His hesitations, retractations, inconsistencies, all proceed from his consciousness of the problems: how do novelistic differ from existential fictions? How far is it inevitable that a novel give a novel-shaped account of the world? How can one control, and how make profitable, the dissonances between that account and the account given by the mind working independently of the novel?

For Sartre it was ultimately, like most or all problems, one of freedom. For Miss Murdoch it is a problem of love, the power by which we apprehend the opacity of persons to the degree that we will not limit them by forcing them into selfish patterns. Both of them are talking, when they speak of freedom and love, about the imagination. The imagination, we recall, is a form-giving power, an esemplastic power; it may require, to use Simone Weil's words, to be preceded by a 'decreative' act, but it is certainly a maker of orders and concords. We apply it to all forces which satisfy the variety of human needs that are met by apparently gratuitous forms. These forms console; if they mitigate our existential anguish it is because we weakly collaborate with them, as we collaborate with language in order to communicate. Whether or no we are predisposed towards acceptance of them, we learn them as we learn a language. On one view they are 'the heroic children whom time breeds / Against the first idea,' but on another they destroy by falsehood the heroic anguish of our present loneliness. If they appear in shapes preposterously false we will reject them; but they change with us, and every act of reading or writing a novel is a tacit acceptance of them. If they ruin our innocence, we have to remember that the innocent eye sees nothing. If they make us guilty, they enable us, in a manner nothing else can duplicate, to submit, as we must, the show of things to the desires of the mind.

I shall end by saying a little more about *La Nausée*, the book I chose because, although it is a novel, it reflects a

philosophy it must, in so far as it possesses novel form,
belie. Under one aspect it is what Philip Thody calls 'an
extensive illustration' of the world's contingency and the
absurdity of the human situation. Mr. Thody adds that it
is the novelist's task to 'overcome contingency'; so that if
the illustration were too extensive the novel would be a
bad one. Sartre himself provides a more inclusive formula
when he says that 'the final aim of art is to reclaim the
world by revealing it as it is, but as if it had its source in
human liberty.' This statement does two things. First, it
links the fictions of art with those of living and choosing.
Secondly, it means that the humanizing of the world's contingency cannot be achieved without a representation of
that contingency. This representation must be such that
it induces the proper sense of horror at the utter difference,
the utter shapelessness, and the utter inhumanity of what
must be humanized. And it has to occur simultaneously
with the *as if*, the act of form, of humanization, which
assuages the horror.

   This recognition, that form must not regress into myth,
and that contingency must be formalized, makes *La Nausée*
something of a model of the conflicts in the modern theory
of the novel. How to do justice to a chaotic, viscously contingent reality, and yet redeem it? How to justify the fictive
beginnings, crises, ends; the atavism of character, which
we cannot prevent from growing, in Yeats's figure, like ash
on a burning stick? The novel will end; a full close may be
avoided, but there will be a close: a fake fullstop, an 'ex-
haustion of aspects,' as Ford calls it, an ironic return to the
origin, as in *Finnegans Wake* and *Comment c'est*. Perhaps
the book will end by saying that it has provided the clues
for another, in which contingency will be defeated, the

novel Marcel can write after the experience described in
Le Temps retrouvé, or Roquentin at the end of *La Nausée.*

But Roquentin's book is only a part of Sartre's book; if
there is here a true novel, an agent of human freedom, it
must be Sartre's, not Roquentin's, which we shall never be
able to read. And evidently Sartre knew about the fallacy
of imitative form: his book, though it surrounds the hero
with images of formlessness, inhumanity, nausea, must not
itself be formless or viscous or inhuman, any more than it
may repeat the formal presumptuousness of the nineteenth-century novel or the arrogant omniscience of Mauriac. It works somewhere between these extremes; in the
homely figure of George Eliot, it is the candle that makes
a pattern of the random scratches on the looking-glass.

This pattern is so humanly important that, humanly speaking, contingency is merely its material; Robbe-Grillet,
thinking of this, remembers Mallarmé's remark that the
world exists *pour aboutir à un livre.* And yet the contingency must be there, or our *as if* will be mere fantasy and
unrelated to the basic human task of imaginative self-
invention.

Sartre began *La Nausée* as an episodic work, and Roquentin's practices reflect this; but the need for structure
grew imperious; it is not enough to write *comme les petites
filles.* Something begins that must have a consonant end:
quelque chose commence pour finir. There will be order.
The first title of the book was *Melancholia,* after the Dürer
engraving. Melancholy is not only an illness; she is also
the patroness of creativity. Alone and desperate among all
those discrete objects—plane and sphere, knife, goat, balance, irregular solid—she will discover an order. This discovery follows the experience of contingency; and it can

never be achieved without imagination, simply by raking among the ashes of the *en-soi,* the dump of the past. That is why Roquentin, when we first encounter him, is a historian. He practises the study of that from which art enables us to escape. We observe his mounting disgust, and finally he rejects M. Rollebon. The association of this historical worthy with the loathsomeness of contingency is inexplicit, achieved by one of those counterfeitings which are the logic of novels, in which collocation represents more than contingency. 'M. de Rollebon m'assomme. Je me lève. Je remue dans cette lumière pâle; je la vois changer sur mes mains et sur la manche de ma veste: je ne peux pas assez dire comme elle me dégoûte.' 'M. de Rollebon bores me. I get up. I move through this pale light; I see it change on my hands and on the sleeve of my coat: I cannot begin to say how much it disgusts me.' How then is he to contain, to transfigure reality? Not by the pathetic mechanical method of the Autodidact, whose alphabetical assimilation of knowledge simply grinds the meaningless ash of contingency even finer; not by the fictions of the *salauds* as he sees them in the art gallery, or of the doctor, who uses conventions as a protection against the anguish of his own freedom. It has to be done by a fiction which is not fraudulent.

Such a fiction is the song, 'Some of these days.' This frail piece is human, creates a human duration, destroys the disorder and the dead time of the world. It contains nothing that is merely a happening; its moments, such as they are, are *aventures*. This is what is needed. There are other hints of the same transfiguration: a card-game has its *aventures,* a life may be looked upon as having them, and indeed as having a structure of them, so that it comes to

resemble a novel ... But when Roquentin experiences the
metaphysical hangover that comes from indulgence in such
thoughts, he tells himself to 'beware of literature.' The
as if of the novel is not so easily to be applied to life. In
life there are no beginnings, those 'fanfares of trumpets'
which imply structures 'whose outlines are lost in the mist.'
In a novel the beginning implies the end: if you seem to
begin at the beginning, 'It was a fine evening in 1922. I
was a notary's clerk in Marommes,' you are in fact beginning at the end; all that seems fortuitous and contingent
in what follows is in fact reserved for a later benefaction
of significance in some concordant structure. This, Roquentin reminds himself, and the young Sartre had reminded himself, distinguishes novels from life, and represents the danger of arguments which confound the two. By
a very imaginative piece of faking, Sartre obliquely illustrates the point in the passage where an 'actual' conversation in a restaurant is couterpointed against a conversation
in *Eugénie Grandet.* They belong to different orders of
life and time. So, too, when Roquentin on his Sunday
walk feels that for once here is *aventure,* what he says is
that this gives him a sense of being which is proper not to
life but to art: 'Il arrive que je suis moi et que je suis
ici ... je suis heureux comme un héros de roman.' Faced
with a perfectly ordinary choice of life, the sense of living
in a novel at once deserts him. But of course he *is* living
in a novel. Thus does Sartre hold together the contingent
and the structure of 'adventures' in a dissonance that leads
to discovery.

The faking by which this is done—I use E.M. Forster's
word, which means something beneficent—is not the faking
of the cowards and the *salauds.* A French critic would here

think of Gide rather than Forster, and Claude-Edmonde
Magny distinguishes between 'cheating'—which is what
the artist does—and 'counterfeit cheating' the cheating in
bad faith of the *salauds*. The novelist cheats by arranging
collocations which, since he is meeting us in a context
which we both understand as we might understand the
nature and the rules of a game, we shall not regard as
fortuitous, in which we shall discover point and rhythm.
La Nausée, like any other novel, has a great many such
contrivances. Finding, like Roquentin, that the root of the
tree is 'beneath all explanation,' we invent, because we are
free, what has the qualities to satisfy the desires of the
mind: a circle, says Roquentin, but he might have said
a novel. There are no circles in reality, and no novels.
When Anny gave Roquentin the kiss which sealed a relationship, she was sitting in a patch of nettles. If life were
'like a work of art' this would not occur; the interesting
thing about *La Nausée* as an enquiry into novel-form is,
of course, that the nettles are there. If the world of words
is to have value, if it is to be distinguished from the protec-
tive fictions of the *salauds* and the nineteenth-century novelists, the nettles must be there.

Why, then, choose, as the leading instance of the satisfactions of art, the song 'Some of these days'? This, of course,
is another piece of faking. The song is a minimal work of
art, the tiniest conceivable check to contingency. In its
three-minute compass the authors made themselves like
heroes of a novel, says Roquentin: 'they washed themselves
of the sin of existing.' They created artificial beginning
and end, a duration minute but human in which all, between those points, is ordered, and so in a fiction chal-
lenges and negates the pure being of the world. If existen-

tialism is a humanism, so is this song, and so is the novel.
Fredric Jameson shows us that *La Nausée* is full of fake
beginnings and endings; individual sentences are apoca-
lyptically charged by fictive ends; and as the narrative
develops the final end begins to exert a gravitational pull
over the adventures and the non-adventures which are thus
given the status of adventures, and so finally distinguish
the work from a non-human nature. Finally there is no
'facticity,' the novel is non-contingent. Otherwise it would
be a babble of unforeshortened dialogue, a random stub-
bing of cigarettes, a collection of events without concordance. Unlike works which belong wholly to the land of
fiction, *La Nausée* represents a world of which this might
be said. Its form has elements of the eidetic, but upon such
images are superimposed new images of contingency. Thus
the inherited form is made, for a time at any rate, acceptable to those whose life behind the screen of words
has not entirely closed their eyes to the nature of the world.
The form of *La Nausée* is an instructive dissonance between humanity and contingency; it discovers a new way
of establishing a concord between the human mind and
things as they are.

When I say that this is characteristic of modern fiction I
do not of course mean that the association of consciousness with nothingness, and of being with a random and
agitated meaninglessness, a disgusting evil paste, is a necessary intellectual position. What is radically characteristic
in Sartre's general position is his treatment of fiction as
deeply distrusted and yet humanly indispensable. In the
novel, where there is an inescapable element of the counterfeit, and an inescapable inheritance of eidetic images,
this mistrust of the indispensable produces that continuous

recherche of which the new theorists speak; the *recherche* itself is not new; though it has been speeded up it is a permanent feature of the genre, which has always been threatened on one side from the need to mime contingency and from the other by the power of form to console. In short, the pressures which require its constant alteration are anguish and bad faith. As to the latter, it proceeds from an uncritical or cowardly adherence to the paradigms. Yet they cannot be dispensed with; and what may seem the necessary impurity of the result is refined by further research. How can we, in a necessarily impure medium, wash ourselves of the sin of existing? Hence the rigour of the theorists, hence novels in which the reader is the only character, and the time so precisely his time that the duration of the book is measured by the time he takes to read it, as the duration of the film *Marienbad* is the ninety minutes passed in watching it.

Extreme rigour could, I suppose, destroy the paradigms and so destroy the novel. I admit that of all the claims made by Robbe-Grillet the most baffling, to me, is that in this new realism the ordinary reader can at last find himself. He repeats this claim in a recent interview printed in *Le Monde* (7-13 Oct., 1965). 'My intention is to make a popular cinema and a popular literature ... I've rediscovered in me the entire arsenal of the popular imagination.' 'Hum!' says the interviewer. I myself find the tone of Sartre's novel to be deeper than that of the books which are in some sense its progeny, if only because he understood that even when the *donnée* is that nothing is given, still not everything can be new. His hero, his beginning and end, his concords, are not in this sense new; they grow in the shadow of earlier beginnings, ends and concords, earlier heroes; had there been no novels in the world to condemn, *La Nausée* could not have been thought of, and it may be that *L'Etre et le néant* could not have been thought of, either.

La Nausée, as I say, has its progeny. The research has gone on. Michel Butor, for example, says that the novel is 'developing within itself those elements which will show how it is related to the rest of reality, and how it illuminates reality; the novelist is beginning to know what he is doing, and the novel to say what it is.' This again seems very characteristic of the stage of 'research' we have reached, the use of fictions for the exploration of fiction. As to reality, this neo-realist (a term which is puzzling, when you think that it is applied not only to Butor but to C. P. Snow) takes nothing for granted. 'Never,' says Mr. Peter Brooks, 'never has the novel been so thoroughly about itself, yet never has it been so engaged with reality.' This is probably excessive; it is a way of calling *L'Emploi du temps* the great modern novel. I should not claim this even for *La Nausée;* but both will be among the books our successors will examine when they consider how little, or perhaps how much, we were, in our day, muddled about the question of what, in our crisis, we could take on trust from the past; and how, being so morbidly aware of the nature and motive of our mendacity, we understood the relations between fiction and reality.

VI

Truly, though our element is time,
We are not suited to the long perspectives
Open at each instant of our lives.
They link us to our losses. . . .

PHILIP LARKIN

Solitary Confinement

In this lecture, which is my last, I shall try to touch upon most of the themes proposed in the earlier ones, though I do not hope to provide in it the marvellous clue that would make all the rest useful and systematic. I could only do that if I were the master described in the poem, that 'more severe, More harassing master' who

> would extemporize
> Subtler, more urgent proof that the theory
> Of poetry is the theory of life
>
> As it is, in the intricate evasions of as,
> In things seen and unseen, created from nothingness,
> The heavens, the hells, the worlds, the longed-for lands.

I have his programme but not his powers. 'Life / As it is, in the intricate evasions of as' is what I am talking about, as best I can; and I am glad that it was in my most recent talk that I discussed Sartre, who knew that fictions, though prone to absurdity, are necessary to life, and that they grow very intricate because we know so desolately that *as* and *is* are not really one. None of our fictions is a supreme fiction.

Our knowing this creates in us, to a most painful degree,

the condition Sartre calls 'need' and Stevens 'poverty.' It
may seem superfluous for me to admit that this poet, at
this time, speaks more urgently and congenially to me than
any other, especially when he speaks of the fictions which
are the proper consolations of human loneliness:

> Natives of poverty, children of malheur,
> The gaiety of language is our seigneur.

This is a way of speaking about a newly realized imaginative poverty in terms of something much older, and which
words will not mitigate; and yet the two situations sometimes run together and blur. To be alone and poor is, in
a sense, everybody's fate; but some people have been alone
and poor in a very literal sense, as most of us have not; and
in solitary confinement some of them have tested the gaiety
of language as a means of projecting their humanity on a
hostile environment. And it is by speaking for a few moments about the book of one such man that I can best
begin to say what I have to say in this final talk.

Christopher Burney, the author of *Solitary Confinement,* was a British agent in occupied France, and the book
begins after his capture, though at a time when he still
found solitude and confinement mere notions with no real
force. What follows is a study of those notions as they become real. I mustn't speak of Burney as if he were *Homo,*
a man in every way able to represent Man. He is abnormally brave, abnormally intelligent, and, it is relevant to
add, upper-class English. His 'project' is coloured by his
education. A man educated on the French pattern, for example, could perhaps not have retained that metaphysical
innocence in the air of which the philosophical fictions of
his captivity attained their own unforeseen shapes. For this

is a book about the world a man invents in real poverty
and solitude, and with as little help as possible from prefabricated formulas. We may, by means of it, come to understand something of the way the world shapes itself in
the mind of true poverty; certainly it will seem right to
think of this author as one of those 'heroic children whom
time breeds / Against the first idea.'

Burney in his cell has two main interests: his appetite
and his thoughts. The first of these he controls in various
ways, playing tricks on it, arranging its slow defeat through
the hours of the day. But the second, his thinking, grows
obsessive. When the man in the next cell tries to communicate by knocking on the wall he is rejected. The
thinker wants no interference with his private figurations.
Burney does not congratulate himself on this. He knew
his own poverty, and might have found value in the knowledge of another's. 'To be able to combine solidarity of
plight with diversity of state must be the highest achievement of the race,' he says, and with much penetration; for
such are the conditions of tragedy. What makes Burney's
book as it were post-tragic is his need to understand his
plight alone. In prison he found himself, paradoxically,
free, within the limits set by hunger and 'the animal lust
to roam.' In that freedom, which was the freedom of acceptance, of true poverty, his mind enabled him to impose
his humanity on the world. Reality is transfigured by this
act, as by an act of love. 'Down on the bedrock,' he writes,
'life becomes a love affair of the mind, and reality merely
the eternally mysterious beloved.' The experience was terrible enough, but to be without the memory of it would be
to forfeit also 'that strange and faithful fraternity of the
windows and those moments when the mind's eye, like

a restless prism, could see reality as no more than an out-
line against the faintly discerned light of truth.' Such are
the consolations of poverty.

The courage and the intellectual integrity of this writer
are far beyond what most of us would expect of ourselves,
and yet we may legitimately look, in the motions of his
mind, for certain characteristic fictions in a pure state. Let
me mention some of these. He is aware that in his solitude
and freedom he has made what he could not have made
among the improvisations of normal life, an objective and
ordered world; remembering *The Franklins Tale*, he calls
this structured world 'ful well corrected,'

> As been his centris and his argumentz
> And his proportioneles convenientz
> For his equacions in every thyng.

Reflecting on the plenitude of this structure, the hero
cannot avoid the problem of evil. He solves it by re-invent-
ing the theology of evil as privation. Pressing on with it, he
rediscovers, in terms of the spectroscope, a Neo-Platonic
philosophy of light. Another problem demands to be faced,
the problem of determinism and free will. Mechanistic explanations are dismissed as fantastic, but as he considers
free will in terms of his own practice (should I eat all my
bread at once, or space it out?) he is forced to conclude
that familiar explanations suffered from a fundamental
misconception: 'it was held that the quality of an act was
determined by an act of volition which supposedly preceded it, whereas I now believed that consciousness of the
value of any action was essentially reflective, and could
only be made crudely to precede the action by a process of
forward imagination, in its turn an act of reflection. . . . /

At this small discovery all the paradoxes of the freedom of human beings over against the omnipotence of God dissolved.' Thus, in poverty, on the bedrock, are the ancient problems restated, and the mind discovers 'what will suffice.'

Burney was required to produce two different varieties of fiction. As well as inventing his own 'equacions in every thyng,' he had to make up stories for the Gestapo. These Gestapo stories had to fulfill certain conditions: without telling the truth, they were required to convince a sceptical audience. They were, in fact, experiments in novelistic *verismo*. They required absolutely plausible character, situation, and dialogue. If they failed, the novelist—we recall that he was literally poor as we are figuratively poor —would be bludgeoned by his critics. The requirement of verisimilitude presses like an evil on his narrative.

'When we arrived near Pau ... an unhealed wound gave my companion so much trouble that we had to rest a while.' I nearly attributed the wound to myself, until I remembered that I had no suitable scar.

Under critical pressure he revises the story somewhat, until an acute but reasonably congenial interrogator can find no fault with it. In a sense, the moment of triumph in this exercise comes when the interrogator, shaking hands, says 'Goodbye, I don't believe a word you've told me.' It is what we might say to the Goncourts, if the street were time and they at the end of the street.

But in the cell again, fictional satisfactions are not to be had by compliance with the paradigms of *verismo;* it is harder to save one's humanity than to save one's life. It is a question, says Burney, of an abstract order obscured

by the 'coarseness of actuality.' This obscuration is to be
inferred not only of the physical world, but also of men,
since every coarse and actual man is 'doubled by an abstract expression of himself.' Since ethics is the relation between this fictional giant and the human animal, ethical
solutions are aesthetic; we are concerned with fictions of
relation. Thus solitude is an 'exercise in liberty' and liberty
is inventing, for all the casualty of life, fictions of relation.

Burney remarks that the movement of his mind often
took him 'to Americas thickly populated by earlier Colum-
buses.' In this true poverty everything had to be re-invented
—even the clock. He needed a clock not because the conventional divisions of time were of pressing importance,
but for reasons closer to those of the monks who first made
them. They needed clocks for the more devout observance
of the offices, Burney because he needed to apprehend the
increasing pressure of an approaching end. As long as his
captivity was story-like in that its moments were to be
given significance by an end, he needed to sense its imminence. 'One does not suffer the passing of empty time,
but rather the slowness of the expected event which is to
end it.' If time cannot be felt as successive, this end ceases
to have effect; without the sense of passing time one is
virtually ceasing to live, one loses 'contact with reality.' So
the prisoner invents a clock, the shadow cast by a gable on
a wall which he can see through the fretted glass of his
high window. Time cannot be faced as coarse and actual,
as a repository of the contingent; one humanizes it by fictions of orderly succession and end.

The final end, death, is something else that cannot be
faced in its inhuman coarseness. Burney could have died
any day, and thought daily of death. But 'Death is a word

which presents no real target to the mind's eye,' he notes. If you imagine yourself being shot, your body being rolled away in a barrow by soldiers, you are cheating yourself by substituting for your own body someone else's, or perhaps an impersonal dummy. Your own death lies hidden from you. This cheating, like the cheating I talked about in my last lecture, can be malignant or benign; in the malignant form it is exemplified by the doctor in *La Nausée,* but in its benign form it is tragedy, which at one time was our way of opening the subject of the hidden death to our reluctant imaginations. Burney goes back behind the tragedy, however, to a simpler eschatology. His fictions have to do with the 'hereafter.' To produce them, he remarks, is a process 'as natural as eating.' The reason for this is that 'we have a vacuum, a perfect secret, proposed to us as our end, and we immediately set about filling it up.'

Paradigmatic fictions, the heaven and hell of his childhood, press themselves upon his thought; but he rejects them. Why? For the reasons I have suggested elsewhere; our scepticism, our changed principles of reality, force us to discard the fictions that are too fully explanatory, too consoling. He develops a sense of the impotence of his fictions, but they continue with a rare truth to type. Lapsing into unclerical naïveté, like the apocalyptists of my first talk, he brusquely invents an end convenient to himself. 'One thing is out of the question. I cannot still be here at Christmas. . . . This was an axiom.' When Christmas comes and he is still there, he notices the necessity of such disconfirmation—'I had made it necessary for me to be wrong by setting the limit in the first place.' Yet he passes Christmas day in the manner of millennarian sects after disconfirmation—calculating this day afresh by estimating the

time needed for the Allies to accumulate the required
number of tanks and landing-craft. 'The essential, though
I did not know it at the time, was to have a boundary
which would make time finite and comprehensible.' It
seems to be an essential, whether one's poverty is real or
figurative; tracts of time unpunctuated by meaning derived
from the end are not to be borne.

All the types of fiction, inherited or invented, naïve or
sophisticated, run together in the mind that seeks freedom
in poverty. They are all part of the world of words, of the
cheat which gives life to the world. Burney considered
language and isolated an aspect of it which reminded him
of a family joke or game, a way of short-circuiting the unintelligible complexities by letting a shared word work in
the varying contexts: love, for example, which is moved up
from the flesh to heaven and down again. He thought a
good deal about the great family jokes which seem mutually contradictory and unstable in meaning, the parables
of the New Testament, for example; they seem in their
conflicting senses to be divorced from the consolatory
gospels in which they are found, calling upon us to make
the effort of concordance; cold, hungry men sitting in a
cell thinking about the prodigal son and the lilies of the
field. Was he the prodigal son or the man who fell among
thieves? One fed hope, the other not. 'The whole Gospel
became more and more a structure of paradoxes, carefully
balanced so that each statement could be invalidated by
another, none having absolute precedence. The lost sheep,
the foolish virgins; the prodigal son and the man with one
talent; they made an impenetrable maze.' Another phrase
in the same book spoke direct sense: 'For all our days are
passed away in Thy wrath; we spend our years as a tale

that is told.' That the concordant tale should include irony
and paradox and peripeteia, that making sense of what
goes to make sense should be an activity that includes the
acceptance of inexplicable patterns, mazes of contradiction,
is a condition of humanly satisfactory explanation.

The epigraph to *Solitary Confinement* is a passage from
the last act of *Richard II*, and I will confess that it never
made such exquisite sense to me before I read Burney's
book.

> For no thought is contended. The better sort,
> As thoughts of things divine, are intermix'd
> With scruples, and do set the word itself
> Against the word:
> As thus—*Come, little ones;* and then again—
> *It is as hard to come, as for a camel*
> *To thread the postern of a small needle's eye.*
> Thoughts tending to ambition, they do plot
> Unlikely wonders: how these vain weak nails
> May tear a passage through the flinty ribs
> Of this hard world, my ragged prison walls;
> And for they cannot, die in their own pride.

These reflections arise out of Richard's 'study' to 'compare / This prison where I live unto the world.' Burney
studies similarly, desiring to find the sense that, when
ambitious thoughts fail, poverty can make of the world,
and the sense of the fictions of poverty. The evidence is
paradoxical, contradictory, the language unstable; the
word is set against the word; above all the appetite for
hope and consolation is invincible. And the question that
must always be asked of whatever offers hope and consolation is equally human and imperious, and without it
nothing will for long make sense: it is whether these ex-

planations and consolations can be 'reconciled with that pan of putrid soup.'

I have been talking about Burney in this discursive way so that we can, if we like, think of his book as a model of a more general solitary confinement, of the fictions and interpretations of human beings 'doing time,' imagining ends and concords. 'Men die because they cannot join the beginning to the end,' but living is trying to do it. We give ourselves meaning by inventing critical time, like the shadow of the gable. Fictions in the end fail under the pressure of what James is said, in his last words, to have called 'at last, the real distinguished thing'; but meanwhile we have our predictive games, our family jokes like *Lear*, our anthropomorphic paradigms of apocalypse; we have a common project, truth in poverty, and a common need, solidarity of plight in diversity of state. The free imagination makes endless plots on reality, attempts to make our proportionals convenient for our equations in everything; our common sense makes us see that without paradox and contradiction our parables will be too simple for a complex poverty, too consolatory to console. Our study, like Richard's, must have a certain complexity and a sense of failure. 'I cannot do it; yet I'll hammer it out,' he says.

So here we are in the middest, and like Richard reinventing the world from inside a prison. Perhaps the autonomy of forms, of which we hear so much in Romantic, Symbolist, and Post-Symbolist criticism, is another reminder of incarceration; perhaps the autonomous forms which are called researches into the autonomy of forms— so much modern poetry, we complain, is about modern poetry, and the new novel is a research into novels—reflect our consciousness that deep in the cell we are using the shadows only, because we have lost the kind of confidence that enabled us to be interested in the apparent facts as well as in the human concords. George Herbert, making metaphors for prayer, called it that which in an hour transformed the six-days world, and he also called it 'a kind of tune.' It was a six-days world because God made it in six days. Music had six notes, one for each day of the creation, of which every tune reflected the harmony. All harmony has this hexameral structure. (Now it may have the structure of twelve tones in the arbitrary sequence invented in the cell.) In much the same way, encyclopaedists used to arrange the whole of human knowledge as a commentary on the six days of creation. To arrange it in terms of an alphabet is to make it conform to an arbitrary human formulation, and one that is obsolete in so far as what is sought in knowledge is concord, proportion, equation, seen from a cell set about by absurdity. The grand universal order of Genesis gave way to the spacious firmament of Newton, and this in turn yields to the subtle complementarities of modern physics; the Gospels submitted to the elaborate harmonies of patristic scholarship, and then to the refined synoptic concordance of the moderns; medieval randomness is transformed by the logic of Aristotelian plot, which is modified by the counter-logical devices of the modern novel, treating time and cause as it is treated by a totalitarian interrogator.

    This, of course, is once again to overstate the case. Even if it were true that the forms which interest us were merely the architecture of our own cells (and it is never quite true) we should have to make allowances for the fact that they do, after all, please us, even perhaps bless us;

and this does not emerge from the tone of what I have just
been saying. Even if we prefer to find out about ourselves
less by encountering what both Williams and Stevens call
'the weather' than by brooding over the darkening recesses
of a Piranesi prison, we feel we have found our subject and
for the moment ourselves; and that for us, as for everybody else, our world has point and structure. We are
conscious of our cheating, and set the word against the
word; but this only means that the concord we still desire
is harder to achieve. When we achieve it, whatever the
circumstances, we feel we have found a reality which is
for the moment at any rate proof against sceptical research; even in an endless, shapeless world this reality has
—to borrow a strange phrase from Josef Pieper—'the character of being-directed-towards-the-End.' What makes the
triumph difficult is that it has to take account of the world
as we experience it; we have a loving-hating affair with
reality, we 'keep coming back to the real'; and this continually impoverishes us because it is at odds with such
concords as we have achieved. So it seems that we move
always with less and less freedom, have less and less use
for inherited wealth.

One reason for this impoverishment, for the growing
difficulty of access to the paradigms, is simply that it is
much harder now than it was even quite recently to imagine a relation between the time of a life and the time of a
world. I talked in my third lecture about this problem in an
earlier form. The modern version is probably much more
upsetting. Fictional paradigms really belong to a world in
which the relation of beginning and end is not too tenuous
—a six-days world, the tight world-scheme of Augustine, the
limited time-scale of Ussher. The quite sudden and enor-

mous lengthening of the scale of history has been far more worrying than the Copernican revolution, of which one hears so much in literary discussion. The six-days world was still perfectly acceptable to intelligent contemporaries of Jane Austen. When it collapsed, the sciences were liberated; what was for the arts a difficulty presented the sciences with a new dimension in which they could luxuriate.

For the sciences one after another turned to the temporal. Geology was first, and then in mid-century Darwin temporalized the spatial classifications of biology. The other sciences, including astronomy, followed. In every case, as Toulmin and Goodfield show in their interesting book, the switch caused some shock; even in Science there can be an emotional attachment to the paradigms. Meanwhile, for everybody, the origin and the end of the world receded. 'No Vestige of a Beginning—no Prospect of an End,' said James Hutton, as early as 1790. For literature and its criticism this created problems we have not yet solved, though it is obviously relevant that the novel developed as the time of the world expanded, and that the facts are related.

We probably have to accept, though without making too much of it, an historical transition, related to this protraction of time, from a literature which assumed that it was imitating an order to a literature which assumes that it has to create an order, unique and self-dependent, and possibly attainable only after a critical process that might be called 'decreation.' (It is a further question whether we may not now have another attempt to shift to the position that no order need be created because the consumer will do this without help if he is given the right encouragement and set in the right situation. But that, I believe, is a mis-

take.) There are many ways of describing this shift, some
of them much too simple and dramatic, full of lamenta-
tion and extravagant inference. For myself, I value some
pages of Earl Wasserman's book, *The Subtler Language,*
as offering an acceptable way of talking about it. In his
terms this transition is a transition from imitation to something more or less like mathematics—from mimesis to
mathesis, or from proposition to surd. Thus the *concordia
discors* of 'Cooper's Hill' reflects the political philosophy
of limited monarchy and implies a universe ordered by
similar checks and balances. The 'subtler language' of 'The
Sensitive Plant' is founded on a different assumption: that
the reality of the senses and the reality of metaphor meet
much more remotely, at some point unimaginable by the
human mind. After such a change the experience of being
isolated from reality, or of moving about in worlds not
realized—or fallings from us, vanishings, of gates that one
desperately clutches in order to disprove their insubstan-
tiality—becomes much more commonplace, much more
frequently a matter for enquiry. Indeed, it is the very
matter-of-factness of Wordsworth that so effectively famil-
iarizes us with a dimensionless, limitless world, resistant
to paradigmatic mimesis, requiring the decreation of old
forms and old ways of speaking, operating in a temporal
mode. He sounds one of the characteristic notes of modern
literature, and begins to make the quasi-spatial mode as
inappropriate to literature as it was becoming to the sciences.

 The discipline of fear is as much a matter of fact as the
discipline of love: it is founded on a sense of remoteness
and estrangement, as the other upon identity and comfort.
One sees why Wordsworth dwelt so much upon those

practically motionless old men, useless, utterly poor, but
somehow identified with the earth they bowed towards,
and so as mysterious as poems. Poems move, for him, out
of fear into a moment of love; but they must acknowledge
the pressure of fact, and so the best of Wordsworth's poems
contain a vertiginous estrangement, a sense of what was
later called the absurd, but transfigure it with joy. This is,
I suppose, a way of stamping the 'characters of great apocalypse' on the terrifying limitlessness of time. The hiding-
places of power, for Wordsworth as for Proust, are the
agents of time's defeat; discovered by involuntary memory,
pure of discursive significance like the girl with the pitcher,
they provide the structure and meaning and pleasure which
constitute our deliverance from the long, meaningless attri-
tion of time. The kinds of life here created Wordsworth
curiously and beautifully speaks of as 'existences . . . like
angels stopped upon the wing by sound.' They belong to
the *aevum*, if you like, sempiternal moments that transcend the giddy successiveness of world-time. These necessary 'conversions of our *Lumpenwelt*,' as Stevens calls
them, are necessarily the work of necessary angels.

One such 'existence' is 'Resolution and Independence,'
to my mind both a very great and a very modern poem.
The peculiar pains that attended the transfiguration of a
commonplace but disquieting incident can be inferred
from Wordsworth's letter of June 14th, 1802, to Sara
Hutchinson, and from Dorothy Wordsworth's Journal for
the early part of May, and for July 2nd of that year. The
actual encounter with the leech-gatherer had occurred
almost two years earlier, in October 1800. The man was
bent double; he had suffered some accident in a cart, which
had left him partly incapacitated. John Wordsworth won-

dered if he was a Jew. His occupation was technologically
more primitive even than hill-farming; and nature, by
growing parsimonious with leeches has reduced him to
utter poverty and at the same time made him a mysterious
part of the landscape. They met the old man near Amble-
side, 'late in the evening, when the light was just going
away.'

The kind of interest this scarecrow figure aroused in
Wordsworth was of the sort that only a poem could satisfy.
He has great difficulty in talking about it, and great difficulty in writing the poem, largely because the old man
talks, and what he says has something to do with the case,
but only in the oblique way that matters of fact have to do
with poems. He needs to put into the poem what the old
man says; of course it is a bit tedious, but how can the
poem work without it? Sara Hutchinson told him she did
not like the end of the poem. He is forced to attempt an
explanation of how she has gone wrong. 'It is in the character of the old man to tell his story in a manner which an
impatient reader must necessarily feel as tedious. But Good
God! Such a figure, in such a place....!' The old man
must say something (say a lot)—it is the fact of the matter
that he does so, irreducibly—and yet he must *be* something
quite different, rather like a poem. For Wordsworth the
task is to explain the power of this image, a man 'travelling
alone among the mountains and all lonely places, carrying
with him his own fortitude and the necessities which an
unjust state of society has entailed upon him.'

But the poem says little about such matters, and is in
fact not 'about' the leech gatherer at all. It is, as Wordsworth says to Sara Hutchinson, about 'a young Poet...
overwhelmed by the thought of the miserable reverses that

have befallen the happiest of men, viz. Poets'; and about
'an interposition of Providence' that gave this young man
a degree of resolution and independence, the power to
contemplate a certain poverty. In the poem the old man
appears at a dream-like moment when the poet's mind and
the morning landscape suddenly darken. His tedious talk
is not attended to, although it is reported in the poem,
until a movement of the poet's mind convinces him that
this may be a peculiar grace, a leading from above; the old
man merges with the pool, and is metamorphosed into the
great stone; the poem is never asking you to attend directly
to the old man, but to its own transfiguration. It has an
end which could pass as the end of a simpler, even of a bad
poem; but here it is a fake, a cheat in the plotting. It says
the poet will henceforth, when he is miserable, be able to
think of this old man. There's always somebody worse off
than yourself.

Yet even in the simpler *faux-naïf* of the *Lyrical Ballads*
Wordsworth is asking the reader to sophisticate the narrative for him. Here he puts everything into the poem. In
fact, its true end is the proof that from time to time, as
now, we are by our own spirits deified; peculiar grace is
the property not so much of grave livers, as of poems. Out
of the intangible age and obscurity of the real world
proceeds this extraordinary moment, with its complex
perspectives of past and future. The poem begins with the
loss of joy, and proceeds through a confrontation with the
mystery of poverty and tedious age—a confrontation without communication, setting the word against the word.

The point is not even Wordsworth's continual anguish,
that nature, which was once as plentiful a provider of
poems as of leeches, will also be leaving it to the poet, as

it has to the leech-gatherer, to 'persevere and find them
where I may.' It is true that here is the first great confrontation of metaphorical with actual poverty, and that this is
what produced the dream and the poem. Hence the extraordinary complexity of the end: the old man's poverty
is unchanged, and he remains motionless on the moor;
there is obviously nothing the poet can do with his except
hope to endure it; and all this is said. But the poem ends
in joy, the joy of its own success in giving a true and original human shape to poverty.

   This poem mimes, as it were, that movement which
Ortega sees in the novel also, out of an objective world of
myth into the subjective consciousness working in time.
That the old world is still represented in it—that you can
find a simple plot in the poem—is testimony to the strength,
perhaps to the indispensability of the paradigms. But they
are transfigured; and one of the forces that go to make this
change is certainly Wordsworth's sense of the past, the
need to find power in temporal 'hiding-places.' The growth
of a poet's mind, for him the true subject of an epic, is no
longer a process of grasping the spatial relations of a six-
days world, turning oneself into a curious and universal
scholar, but the process of finding oneself, by some peculiar
grace, in lost time.

   In this dark backward there are no limits for the form
to imitate. It was a preoccupation of De Quincey's, this
absence of a given design, this new power of fortuity. In
this situation he called time a 'greater mystery' than space,
and as J. Hillis Miller explains in his fine essay on this
author, the longing for an experience which would charge
the present moment with the intangible powers of past
and future, was a longing satisfied by what he called 'the

apocalypse of the world within me'—a fake end, when time
shall be no more, produced by opium. This is the triumph
over time; in his attempts to reflect in syntax and argument this defeat of successiveness, De Quincey looks forward to many later artists, to the poetry of the apocalyptic
image and the spatialized moment, even to that rescue
from *chronos* of sempiternal events which we find in
Proust. Here are anticipations of a literature of perpetual
crisis, as in Kafka, who (in William Phillips's phrase) 'loads
each particular experience with the sum of all experience.'
But De Quincey, longing for external evidence of such
sempiternity, admitted that one cannot write against the
text of time a perpetually iterated *stet;* he sinks back 'into
an impotent misery,' says Mr. Miller, 'a misery in which
the self is once again a solitary point,' and when the 'vision-
ary morning life' consents to be summoned up, it is 'relived
on a background of funereal darkness.' Certainly De
Quincey saw the horror, where others see the depth, of the
prison of modern form, the place where we accept the
knowledge that our inherited ways of echoing the structure
of the world have no concord with it, but only, and then
under conditions of great difficulty, with the desires of our
own minds.

   Let me return a moment to Christopher Burney in his
cell. He discovered this image of modern art: inconceiva-
ble diversity of state without solidarity of plight. What
kind of fictions would you expect from this? Fictions as
far as possible from ritual, certainly, or even from the
forms that derive from ritual, such as tragedy. As for
verismo, in these circumstances it is strictly for the police.
Burney's fictions were of time, and of a world where the
word is set against the next word. Such fictions will be

complex, certainly, proof against discursive reduction; but
they will live in time and change, because these are necessary to the sense of life, the more so when the spatial diagrams of the world have given way to temporal ones.
Which brings me, finally, to the defence of time and
change.

In so far as there is an art of the timeless prison, it is
poetry; that so many critical techniques are also of the
timeless prison may be historically accounted for by the
fact that 'formal' criticism is much more closely associated
with poems than novels. *The Waste Land* is intended to be
outside time, though of course it has a temporal aspect;
this is progressive form, as Kenneth Burke talks about it, a
'temporizing of essence.' Novels, however, no matter how
much they shift time, put slices of it layer on layer in search
of intemporal concord, are always in some way bound to
what Sartre calls its 'manifest irreversibility.' Their beginnings, middles, and ends, however refined, however dis-
torted from the paradigm, will always join it somewhere.

It is a familiar problem. 'Beginnings are always trouble-
some,' says George Eliot; and 'conclusions are the weak
point of most authors,' she adds, noting that 'some of the
fault lies in the very nature of a conclusion, which is at
best a negation.' Fielding, who detested epistolary form,
allowed it one advantage: it set the writer free 'from reg-
ular beginnings and conclusions.' History separates from
chronicle, providing its own structures; the novel separates
from the simple narrative. The problem of beginnings and
ends in a form which, paradigmatically, imitates the form
of the world, is created. So the best beginnings are the best
faked, as in the perfect opening sentence of *A Passage to
India;* in the irony of the opening of *Wuthering Heights*

(the 'solitary neighbour I shall be troubled with'). <u>Ends</u> <u>are ends only when they are not negative but frankly trans-</u> <u>figure the events in which they were immanent.</u>

The end of *Anna Karenina*, for instance: it recapitulates the domestic beginning. You remember the opening: 'All happy families are alike but an unhappy family is unhappy after its own fashion. Everything had gone wrong in the Oblonsky household. . . .' A thousand pages later, in the Levin household, 'everyone is in the most amiable frame of mind.' Levin is listening to Koznyshev's theory about a new world epoch inaugurated by the Slavonic races when he is summoned to the nursery by his wife. On the way he thinks of other large arguments concerning God and providence, problems to which he has not formulated the answer. In the nursery his wife merely wants to tell him that the baby can now recognize them. A thing which had formerly seemed to Levin so pitiable that it merely added to the general stock of anxiety had become a loved person. On the way back to his guests in the drawing room Levin again worries about God, and the salvation of the heathen. But the kind of truth he has just seen in the nursery is the only kind in his grasp. Now Kitty interrupts him, sends him on an errand. He does not tell her he has made a discovery, of the solidarity of human plight; instead, happy as all families are happy, his will give him the same kind of life, full of contradictions, of words set against words, prayer and quarrelling; now he can say this: 'my whole life, independently of anything that can happen to me, every minute of it is no longer meaningless as it was before, but has a positive meaning of goodness with which I have the power to invest it.' In this conclusion, Levin speaks for the book; as much as he, it needs a happy family at its close; it needs characters who cease to be things and become persons; it needs to be invested by a power which will transfigure the verisimilar events of which its temporal course is made. And as for Levin, this power is a human power providing a human truth, as inaccurate maybe as our way of talking about the stars or as the prophecies of apocalyptic pan-Slavism. Perhaps, as Dostoevsky guessed, Levin will 'destroy his faith again . . . tear himself on some mental nail of his own making.' But we are concerned with the end, not of Levin, but of *Anna Karenina*, with the humanly necessary fake. 'Really, universally,' says James in the preface to *Roderick Hudson*, 'relations stop nowhere, and the exquisite problem of the artist is eternally to draw, by a geometry of his own, the circle in which they shall happily *appear* to do so.' And he goes on thus, very aptly to our purpose: 'He is in the perpetual predicament that the continuity of things is the whole matter for him, of comedy and tragedy; that this continuity is never broken, and that, to do anything at all, he has at once intensely to consult and intensely to ignore it.'

Here is the problem, the consulting and ignoring of continuity and especially the successiveness of time. Ignoring it, we fake to achieve the forms absent from the continuous world; we regress towards myth, out of this time into that time. Consulting it, we set the word against the word, and create the need for difficult concords in our fictions. But we ignore it at great peril; when, as Virginia Woolf puts it, 'the skin of the day has been cast into the hedge,' the novel is dead. Joyce's day in *Ulysses* retains plenty of skin; it seems very doubtful that he 'proceeded on the assumption that a unified spatial apprehension of his work would ultimately be possible,' as Joseph Frank claims, for the book is full of coincidences that are non-significant, and there is a real indeterminacy in character which can only imply, as Arnold Goldman remarks, a 'thickening web of contingency'—we are 'forced to carry ultimate explanations to the novel's end.' There is a polarity of static and dynamic; there is a mimesis of change, potential, as well as a structure of the kind we call spatial. As the book goes forward the Odyssean design is less and less dominant; the data which limit Stephen's freedom are diminished. Time and change, to the disgust of Wyndham Lewis, thrust back into the arts; the assault on temporality in fiction succeeded in the 'luminous statis' of the Vortex, but it does not succeed with fiction. 'Our Vortex does not suck up to life,' said *Blast*. But the novel has to, in however refined a way; it cannot banish time as Lewis banished it, even to the degree that poems and criticism can; of course it cannot banish the form we like to think of as spatial, either.

I believe that Burney in his cell, watching the shadow of the gable, and including it in his attempts to make sense, makes more sense than spatial form. This has grown very systematic and elaborate since Joseph Frank first named it and studied its history. His 'new Laocoon' implied that although books are inescapably of the element of time, their formal organization is to be apprehended as spatial; one would read them twice, as it were, once for time and once for space. And Frank says quite rightly that a good deal of modern literature is designed to be apprehended thus. He adds of Proust that he 'stamps his novel indelibly with the form of time,' as he promised to do; but that by various means he also 'forces the reader to juxtapose disparate images spatially' so that we get what Ramon Fernandez called a 'spatialization of time and memory.'

Used in this way, 'spatialization' is one of those metaphors which we tend to forget are metaphorical, like the metaphor of organic form. Marcel, when he considers those happenings which gave him the clue to his experience, and restored, as he says, his faith in literature, is not talking about spatial form. The portents of his climactic day make sense for him by a benefaction of meaning; the end makes a concord with what had preceded it. But the experiences reserved for permanent meaning, carried out of the flux of time, surely do not make a pattern in space; they punctuate that order of time, free of contingency, in which only the ur-novel wholly exists, the *durée* if you like, or the *aevum*.

Forms in space, we should remember, have more temporality than Lessing supposed, since we have to read them in sequence before we know they are there, and the relations between them. Forms in time have an almost negligible spatial aspect (the size of the book). Their interrelations had much better be studied by reference to our usual ways of relating past, present and future—ways upon which I touched in my second talk—than by the substitution of a counterfeit spatial for the temporal mode. The equation 'between an exodus and return in time through reversible space and an exodus and return in space through reversible time' is, as we are told in the 'Ithaca' section of *Ulysses,* unsatisfactory.

We have our vital interest in the structure of time, in the concords books arrange between beginning, middle, and end; and as the Chicago critics, with a quite different emphasis, would agree, we lose something by pretending that we have not. Our geometries, in James's word, are required to measure change, since it is on change, between remote or imaginary origins and ends, that our interests are fixed. In our perpetual crisis we have, at the proper seasons, under the pressure perhaps of our own end, dizzying perspectives upon the past and the future, in a freedom which is the freedom of a discordant reality. Such a vision of chaos or absurdity may be more than we can easily bear. Philip Larkin, though he speaks quietly, speaks of something terrible:

> Truly, though our element is time,
> We are not suited to the long perspectives
> Open at each instant of our lives.
>   They link us to our losses . . .

Merely to give order to these perspectives is to provide consolation, as De Quincey's opium did; and simple fictions are the opium of the people. But fictions too easy we call 'escapist'; we want them not only to console but to make discoveries of the hard truth here and now, in the middest. We do not feel they are doing this if we cannot see the shadow of the gable, or hear the discoveries of dissonance, the word set against the word. The books which seal off the long perspectives, which sever us from our losses, which represent the world of potency as a world of act, these are the books which, when the drug wears off, go on to the dump with the other empty bottles. Those that continue to interest us move through time to an end, an end we must sense even if we cannot know it; they live in change, until, which is never, *as* and *is* are one.

Naturally every such fiction will in some measure repeat others, but always with a difference, because of the changes

in our reality. Stevens talks about the moment out of poverty as 'an *hour* / Filled with expressible bliss, in which I
have / No need.' But the hour passes; the need, our interest in our loss, returns; and out of another experience of
chaos grows another form—a form in time—that satisfies
both by being a repetition and by being new. So two
things seem to be true: first, that the poet is right to speak
of his giant as 'ever changing, living in change'; and secondly, that he is right to say that 'the man-hero is not the
exceptional monster, / But he that of repetition is most
master.' Moreover, he is right about another thing, which
for us who are medium men, living in a reality which is
always February, is the most important of all. If he were
wrong here we should have to close up our books of poetry
and read somebody on Necessity:

> Medium man
> In February hears the imagination's hymns
> And sees its images, its motions
> And multitudes of motions
>
> And feels the imagination's mercies....

Epilogue

This new edition of *The Sense of an Ending,* prompted by the approach of the millennium, gives me an opportunity to look back to the occasion of its first publication, and to make a few comments on its subject. They will necessarily reflect some of the differences brought on by great changes in the world at large, and will no doubt also be influenced by differences of perspective inevitable in an author thirty-five years older than when he first wrote the book. Over these years I have often thought about the topics it addressed, and attended to criticism of it, but I must say that I have not found good reason to disown it entirely.

In the autumn of 1965, when I gave the lectures which make up *The Sense of an Ending,* the end of the present millennium still seemed far in the future; but no one could ignore the imminence of events that could without too much exaggeration be characterized as apocalyptic. The Cuban missile crisis and the assassination of President Kennedy were quite recent events, the Cold War remained very cold, and words like "megadeath" were common currency; that this word does not appear in the second edition of the *Oxford English Dictionary* (1989) may hint at a change of mood, a lessening, however temporary, of apocalyptic anxiety after that time. The war in

Vietnam was rapidly escalating. The race riots at Watts, which cost many lives, seemed to prefigure even more disastrous upheavals of the same kind. It seemed more than merely possible that there was a bad time coming, possibly a terminally bad time. All of which at least goes to show that the apocalypse can flourish on its own, quite independently of millennia. In some form or another its terrors and apprehensions can threaten us at any time. The possibility of personal disaster is, after all, never quite absent from our lives, and if anything is needed to give additional substance to our anxieties, the world, at whatever period, will surely provide it.

There is nothing new about this situation. I well remember a faculty member at Bryn Mawr taking issue with my remark that our fears, concentrated on nuclear war, could hardly be more acute than those of our ancestors, for they too experienced or expected terrifying manifestations, dreadful omens, armies in the sky and so forth, and were repeatedly warned, on authority they were unlikely to question, of the inescapable terrors of the Last Days. My friend at Bryn Mawr insisted that there was an important and obvious difference between us and these medieval persons: our fears were real; Okinawa and Nagasaki had been destroyed, far more devastating bombs had been successfully tested, and we had seen something of what they could do. In short, we all had an informed and horrifying idea of the consequences of a nuclear attack, whereas their terrors, backed by no such hard evidence, were only fantasies.

This argument seemed and still seems to me to be palpably wrong. Who supposes that fantasies cannot be terrible? Terror does not depend upon an accurate estimate of the threat. That should be obvious to all who have experienced childhood fears; and of the fears that assail us later in life, some no doubt are real enough, but some, as we discover with relief, are groundless. So the prospect of the end of the world, accompanied by the last judgment and the tortures of damnation, vividly represented in many churches and enforced by terrific sermons, must in any case have been real enough, incontrovertible even, not a bit less certain than the fate we believed to be threatening us.

We now seem to be less appalled by our knowledge of the Bomb than we were in the sixties. Perhaps we have simply grown accustomed to the idea; or perhaps the end of the Cold War has eased minds all too ready to welcome such remission. Whether we are right to feel so complacent is quite another matter. The question is not relevant to my concerns in this book, so I won't venture into it, except to remark that our calm is a further demonstration that there is no *intrinsic* connection between apocalypse and millennium. We had the terrors when the millennium was hardly in our thoughts, and must now contemplate the millennium with far less immediate pressure from the terrors, though they will undoubtedly return in force. They belong to no particular time and can indifferently take the form they assumed for us thirty-odd years ago, or the form they were given five hundred years earlier, say in the frescoes of Signorelli at Orvieto, or in those of Michelangelo in the Sistine Chapel; or in some other form we, with the cooperation of the world we must live in, can now give them, and will continue to give them long after the dawn of the second millennium is only a memory. After all, 1666 and 1842 and many other dates have been taken by the initiate, on high authority, to be the dates destined to accommodate the End, though to the outsider they might seem to have been arrived at quite randomly, or by absurd calculations acceptable only to tragically or farcically misguided and ignorant people.

However, before one rejoices at this clean separation of the two it is necessary to add that the historical associations of these ideas, apocalypse and millennium, however obviously the products of untutored imaginative activity, have by custom, and the age-long and not yet extinct authority of the Bible, grown quite strong. This is why so many fundamentalist Christians intend to collapse millennium into apocalypse and celebrate AD 2000, or Y2K as they sometimes call it, as the date after which time shall be no more. It is reported that many mean to visit Israel (some, as I read in January 1999, have already arrived there) in order to watch it all happening at Armageddon (now Megiddo), or even to do what they can to make it happen as closely as possible to the prophetic account provided, in admittedly vaporous allegorical detail, by St. John. As Bernard McGinn remarks, "The conflict of interpretations between academic readings [of Revelation] carried on in schools of divinity and religion and in departments of English on the one hand, and the mass of general readers [influenced, for example, by Hal Lindsey or Billy Graham] on the other , is probably greater now than ever before."[1] One can only suppose that there will be a mass demonstration of the phenomenon identified, on a smaller scale, by Leon Festinger, as reported in the opening chapter above: when the prediction is disconfirmed a few weak souls may abandon fundamentalist prophecy, but most will return to the biblical numbers, which offer an indefinitely wide predictive scope, and come up with another date, this time unrelated to the millennium.

One text always seems to be overlooked: "But of that day and that hour knoweth no man, no, not the angels which are in heaven, neither the Son, but the Father" (Mark 13:32 Matt. 24:30). Mark gives a vivid account of the "tribulation" that must precede the end, but will say no more than that the end, though assuredly nigh, is not yet. The caution is repeated in

Act 1:7: "It is not for you to know the times or the seasons, which the Father has put in his own power." Even the prediction of the author of Revelation (in the first words of his book) is not specific; he undertakes only to show what must shortly come to pass, though he admittedly goes on to offer a range of mathematical puzzles that have traditionally invited and frustrated exact predictions. It is a curious game, an exercise in literalistic and numerological interpretation imposed upon the deliberate obscurities of a text written in a Jewish tradition of opaque apocalypses, apt to offer what look like clues but always withholding answers. The game need never be ended, and it has seemed important enough to be played at one level by mathematicians of genius, like Napier, inventor of logarithms, or Newton, and at another by any ignoramus with access to a Bible. Almost any prediction can be justified by reference to Revelation, and, if needed, assistance is at hand from the Old Testament prophecies of Daniel and from other apocalyptic texts in the gospels and epistles. And the appeal of the decimal, supported by the Jewish equation one day equals a thousand years, ensures that millennial dates may be brought in as valid counters in the game, this being the point at which apocalypse and millennium may merge. For dates must be predicted, and if a millennial date is within range it will serve very well.

It seems unlikely that the medieval laity concerned itself with the quest for a calendar date on which the end of the world would come. The certainty of that end was so urgently insisted upon by their betters that they probably just thought it imminent, without putting a date on it; and insofar as it was a grand image of each individual's own death and judgment it was, after all, exactly that: imminent. The learned might work on the biblical sums and come up with a convenient date, fairly close to their own and not necessarily millennial. Few people, relatively speaking, have the good fortune, if that is what it is, to live to see such a date as 1000 or 2000; but all, regardless of their *floreats*, have to come to terms with a personal apocalypse. As St. Augustine observed, anxieties about the end are, in the end, anxieties about one's own end; he was long before me in suggesting that apocalypse, once imaginable as imminent, had the capacity to become immanent instead.

Since most people, one supposes, understand that the connection between apocalypse and millennium is fortuitous, the mildly apocalyptic stir of anxiety or interest induced by the year 2000 is (except for fundamentalists, who in any case are confident that they will be carried off to safety before Armageddon) only a faint, modern vestige of an older and greater dread, belonging to a vastly different understanding of the world and of time. The date certainly looks strange after we have an ingrained habit of starting dates with 19__, and it may be that we shall welcome the year 2000 as the Scots at Hogmanay welcome a first-foot, a person required to be a stranger bearing gifts symbolic of heat and nourishment.

What we cannot say is that the millennium is somehow more real, more a part of the nature of things, than the apocalypse we dismiss as a fantasy. The millennium is the result of a very long series of manipulations of an entirely artificial chronology. We know the history of the world has been inconceivably longer than the 6000 years so long accepted on biblical authority, and we also know that AD 2000 is two thousand years after nothing in particular. That we should grant the date more than merely calendrical importance is a consequence of something that goes much deeper, and this fact is worth some consideration in the context of the book to which this is an appendix. The reason why any date, almost any excuse, is good enough to trigger some apocalyptic anxiety is that apocalypse, even in its less lurid modern forms, still carries with it the notions of a decadence and possible renovation, still represents a mood finally inseparable from the condition of life, the contemplation of its necessary ending, the ineradicable desire to make some sense of it. And here the myth of millennium (for it has, like other beliefs mentioned above, degenerated from fiction to myth) can offer some help to apocalypse, understood in this broader sense.

The blending together of millennium and apocalypse is primarily attributable to the Bible, where apocalyptic prophecy is often associated, however obscurely, with certain dates or spans of time. Psalm 90:4 ("A thousand ages in thy sight are but as yesterday when it is past") and 2 Peter 3:8 ("one day is with the Lord a thousand years, and a thousand years as one day") authorized the assumption that since God created the world in six days the history of his creation would run to 6000 years, and be followed by a millennial sabbath analogous to the seventh day on which God rested. This was an idea that conferred a special dignity on millennial dates. A span of a thousand years was a sixth of all the time there ever was or ever would be, and of course the sixth span had to be the last. The moment of moving out of one span of time, into another, especially as there might not be another to move into, remained crucially interesting. Obviously there was a need for means of measuring historical time, so that such critical moments could be identified.

The evolution of the calendar by which we measure historical time has been a very laborious and complicated matter.[2] The calendar of Julius Caesar had to be progressively improved as it fell more and more out of kilter with the natural year. There was a long-needed revision by Pope Gregory XIII in

1582 (it is still not quite perfect, for its year is about twenty-six seconds fast, and in due course it will have to be revised again). The religious uses of the calendar had to be worked out. The sixth century saw the beginnings of the system still in use, by which dates are calculated in terms of years before and after the birth of Christ, BC and AD. Here were more flaws, caused partly because it came in before the calculators knew about zero, which should be the date of the years between BC 1 and AD 1.

There are still complaints about the calendar, about the uneven distribution of days per month, about the fact that days of the week fall differently in successive years, and so on. The BC/AD arrangement is awkward, involving counting down on one side and counting up on the other. Several centuries passed before the system achieved anything like general acceptance in the Christian world, and of course at first it applied only there. Still, it worked reasonably well, both for religious and mundane purposes. Subsequently it was secularized (indeed many people, especially in the United States, now amend the prefixes to BCE (before the common era) and CE). But since we still date all history from a starting point that is also the inaugural date of a religion—a religion strongly associated with political and imperial power—there remains a relationship between the calendar and the prophecies derived from that religion and its sacred books.

It is an important consideration that our starting point was also the moment when the consequences of the Fall were remedied by the Incarnation. A new series of time began, and it was somehow, at least potentially, of a different quality; the Incarnation entailed the intervention of God into human time, after which nothing could be quite as it was. No year could be as important as the first, though for people accustomed to the

decimal system of counting, centurial and millennial dates
serve not only as clear invitations to celebrate with special
vigor the birthday of Christ, but also as memorials of that huge
transvaluation of time. They also celebrate the key moment of
renewal, the moment when decadence ends and renovation
may begin; the moment offering an occasion for personal or
general improvement. The end of a century or a millennium,
even more than the end of a year, can be thought of as such an
occasion, and one that cannot be repeated in a lifetime; it may
offer an end to the long process of decline, and bring in a new
order of time; it is a fitting moment for cleansing and renovation. Thus the millennium is a calendrical fiction that makes
available new attitudes to time and its passage. To the religious,
this may be accepted as a by-product of something over-
whelmingly important, the divine descent into history. Others
may say that its interest lies rather in the manner in which it
facilitates the development and expression of ideas or senti-
ments already existing in the human mind.

   In support of the latter hypothesis it can of course be argued
that the need and desire for a new start may long predate
Christianity. One might refer to earlier celebrations of the turn
of time, marked by more or less spectacular events in the natural world: the lunar cycle, the procession of the seasons, especially the rebirth represented by spring. The calendar, once the
concept was entertained, adopted and affected such celebrations, as we know from the protracted arguments in the early
church concerning the day of Easter. The practice of marking
the turn of time is certainly ancient, and it survives to this day.
We may treat January 1 (a date which acquired importance for
us only after it came to be thought of as opening the new year,
displacing March 25) as of only secondary significance, and
liturgically it is not a major feast, only the feast of the

Circumcision, and merely one of the the days of Christmas. But it's a special day, all the same, and it has a faintly pagan aura. When inhabitants of the Celtic fringe make it their principal winter celebration they may be vaguely conscious of its pagan origins, and may even remember that it inaugurates the month of Janus, the god with faces at the back as well as the front of the head. Thus, looking both before and behind, to what is ending and what is beginning, he presides over the turn of time. And if a new year is worth a god and answers to such a complexity of demands, it goes without saying that a new millennium must be.

When we celebrate these transitional moments, after whatever fashion, we are following the example of many generations of ancestors. Such moments punctuate and measure our time and our lives; they are the ancestors or congeners of the many other fictions we use to make sense of our worlds and our lives. For to make sense of our lives from where we are, as it were, stranded in the middle, we need fictions of beginnings and fictions of ends, fictions which unite beginning and end and endow the interval between them with meaning.

I called these "concord-fictions," taking them to be like the plots of novels, which often end with an appearance of concord, or, in modern fiction, a denial of it in the interests of what I called "clerkly scepticism." There have been protests against some of my arguments, especially the one that distinguishes between myth and fiction, the former being a fiction not consciously held to be fictive, and, as I tried to explain, dangerous for that reason. There were also complaints about the tick-tock paradigm in the second chapter.[3] I feel reasonably unrepentant about having started these hares, since, fictive themselves, they have enabled me and others to think differently about fiction in general. Some of the notions here expressed received learned development from Paul Ricoeur in his long study of time and narrative, and from Wolfgang Iser, who develops and qualifies the idea of the concord fiction, making it, I think, more useful.[4] And fictions ought to be made as useful as possible before they are discarded (Chapter 3).

Perhaps because it was written thirty-odd years too early for me to be much bothered about the millennium, *The Sense of an Ending* was only incidentally concerned with calendrical issues, its central interest being rather eschatological, in a very general way concerned with Last Things, and consonant with Blake's remark quoted in the epigraph to the first chapter: the vision of the Last Judgment "is Seen by the Imaginative Eye of Every one according to the situation he holds." For Blake this vision occurs only when "Imagination, Art & Science & all Intellectual Gifts ... are look'd upon as of no use ..."[5] It occurs, that is, at a moment of crisis or transition, and looks forward to a renovation following a decadence, here represented as the decay of the life of the mind. Above all, the vision depends on the imaginative powers of every individual; it is a common theme, like death, or perhaps it cannot finally be distinguished from the idea of death, as death may be considered by "Every one" under conditions of creative privacy.

Such visions of the last judgment, in whatever form they appear to the individual, evidently belong to a different order of time than the merely successive. We ought to take account of this and of many other departures from clock time, from mere succession. This is what Macbeth meant by "success" when he said it would be good "to trammel up the consequence and catch/With his surcease *success*"—he was thinking what a good thing it would be for him if time would only stop, that consequences would stop the moment he killed Duncan. But as

Macbeth understood well enough, that wasn't going to happen; as long as he lived there would be consequences.
Shakespeare remarked elsewhere that "Time, though it 'takes
survey of all the world, must have a stop,"[6] but it is only by
one's own death that one makes this closure possible. Murder
simply doesn't work; it may give a certain distinction or eleva-
tion to the moment of the crime, make of it an evil *kairos*, but
afterwards one has to live day by day, now encumbered with
consequences, with guilt and fear, with the terrible dreams. A
murder is an important moment, no doubt, standing apart
from ordinary moments, but the murderer is unlikely to celebrate its anniversaries.

Birthdays, anniversaries, saints' days, are (fictively, by a
benefaction, so to speak, of *kairos*) distinguished from all other
days. The year of a millennium is certainly such a day. In one
sense there had never before been such a year, such a date: AD
2000 is a celebration open to all, as AD 1000 was not, since it
was identifiable mainly by the literate.

I continue to be interested in the idea, mentioned in my second chapter, that within human time one can distinguish between the *chronos* of mere successiveness and the *kairos* of high
days and holidays, times or seasons that stand out (red-letter
days, as one used to stay) as belonging to a different temporal
order. It was my belief that in referring to the sound of a clock
not as "tick-tick" but as "tick-tock" we substitute a fiction for
the actual acoustic event, distinguishing between genesis of
"tick" and apocalypse of "tock," and conferring on the interval
between them a significance it would otherwise lack. The fictive end purges the interval of simple chronicity. It achieves a
"temporal integration"—it converts a blank into a *kairos*,
charges it with meaning. So it can be argued that we have here
a tiny model of all plots. It is even possible to extend this no-

tion of fictive transformation to argue that the New Testament was not simply a new set of narratives and instructions but the "tock" answering the initial "tick" of the Old, moving the whole Bible out of mere successiveness and, in giving it an entirely new plot, converting the Bible from *chronos* into *kairos*.

I see I was a little timid about this idea and drew back from the claim that the relation between the Testaments was so fully typological that such claims could be made with real confidence. Yet it cannot be denied that when the Christians took over the Jewish Bible they converted it into another book entirely, an extraordinary act of fictive imagination.

I have changed my view of this transformation. From the Christian point of view the true relation of the Testaments really *is* typological; the Passion narratives have their narrative origins in Old-Testament types, the point I backed away from but later came to accept.[7] There would be little reason to mention this change of mind were it not that my earlier position tended to obscure the importance of the transformation effected by the evangelists: their account of the ending (and they believed that they were living near the end, that upon them the ends of the world were coming [1 Cor. 10:11]) is what makes the whole Bible a book of which the later sense could not have been predicted before this ending was supplied. The book is now a whole, starting from "in the beginning" and, since Revelation is placed last in the book, ending at the end, so that the whole vast collection has unity, makes one sense, conferred precisely by this transformative fiction. The end-less successiveness of the original narratives is abolished; there is a peripeteia that turns everything around and gives sense and completeness (*pleroma*, as I called it) to the whole work.

We should not think of this style of transformation as unique. The interpretation of narrative usually involves some sort of transformative manoeuvre, as when we find or seek allegorical meanings or make "symptomatic" readings that discover what, under all the appearances, can be taken to be a true sense of the text. The habit is an ancient one; a modern form of it is the psychoanalyst's interpretation, when, in what seems to be tedious succession of the analysand's discourse, something significant is disclosed to expert attention, something the hoped-for existence of which is a prime if not the only reason for listening to all the rest. So, in the disposable, time-bound talk of the patient, there is exposed what truly exists in another realm of time, an intemporal sign that may take its part in a pattern that has nothing to do with *chronos*; it is basic doctrine that the unconscious knows nothing of time. Nor has it anything to do with eternity; it inhabits that medium between, which could be called *aevum*.

This is an awkward word, and I believe that is one reason why it was probably the least discussed of the ideas I put forward in 1967. Yet the concept still strikes me as one to be taken seriously. Of course I used it in an extended sense which may seem fanciful, and my belief in it cannot be of the kind it elicited in medieval theology. The angels required their own order of time because they were not pure being, yet were (on most interpretations) immaterial, acting in time yet not of it, any more than they participated in God's eternity. Immutable, not subject to time, they were nevertheless capable of acts of will and intellect, by which change is produced in time. St. Thomas gave the necessary idea of a *medium inter aeternitatem et tempus* this name, *aevum*. This idea had a long history and was useful to legal theorists dealing, for example, with monarchies (when the king dies his dignity survives and belongs to the *aevum*), or with corporations, which have a kind of immortality since they survive their mortal members.

But it can also be applied to what I called "men in certain postures of attentiveness." I tried to extend this idea to the time of characters in novels and so to illuminate the relations between our sense of real time and our concessions to the different temporal structure of novels, with their inevitable preference for *kairos* over *chronos*, to which nevertheless some concessions or gestures must be made.

Perhaps this development of a fiction into an instrument for the interpretation of fictions might seem a little too elaborate; but the purpose of heuristic fictions, regardless of their contents, is to do their job and be dropped; they are "consciously false." I now believe that *aevum* can do even more work than I originally proposed for it, since we can use it to mean the realm of the *kairoi* not only of stories but of the ordinary human life, and even of the calendar.

The original text of this book contains other arguments and deals with several topics to which I have not, in this epilogue, returned. With what I said about them I am generally still in agreement, and emphatically so with my remarks about Shakespeare and Spenser in the third chapter, and I do not regret the devoted attention paid to Christopher Burney in the final chapter. Rereading the whole book I am struck by the ubiquity of Wallace Stevens. It is true that my head was full of Stevens at the time, so much so that my friend the late John Wain, another admirer of Stevens, described the book as a love letter to the poet. Since those days I have kept up my acquaintance with Stevens and if I did write him a love letter I'm not for a moment ashamed of it, and have in fact done him homage in several later works. He remains the poet who, when the mood is right, speaks most directly to me; he understood fictions, and he understood the radiance associated with the notion of *kairos*, a radiance he sometimes associated with the

seasons (*kairos*, after all, means "season"). He also understood
that the imagination is always at the end of an era; and that
"One day enriches a year." One knows what he might have said
about the millennium: it will serve as an image of those days
different from all the other days. He wrote of midsummer that
it was

> ... the last day of a certain year
> Beyond which there is nothing left of time.

It could be any day on which succession seems to stop, for him
any day of present blessedness, of poetry and apotheosis. The
permanence of such days or moments is illusory; as the poet
Les Murray says of the poetic experience, "We can have it repeatedly, and each time timelessly, but we find it hard to take
in steadily, to sustain."[8] And of course the day or the moment
may, in its difference, be far from blessed.

I suggested that books are "fictive models of the temporal
world." Although this remark leaves a great deal more to be
said (see Iser on the importance of the imaginary[9]) there is an
important qualification, that the adequacy of such models depends on their paying respect to "real time"; that is, they will
not work as pure *kairos*, since that would be false to our sense
of temporality, a prevailing successiveness of which we all are,
given that we are sane, as aware as we are of the distinctive-
ness of *kairoi*. These moments I rather primly identified as
characterized by "regressive pleasure," believing that the story
needs a dose of reality to make it acceptable, a dose, I said,
that has needed to be increased as time goes by. The crucial
point is that in much the same way as the end of the Bible
transforms all its contents, our sense of, or need for, an ending transforms our lives "between the *tick* of birth and the *tock*

of death," and stories simulate this transformation but must not do so too simply.

The question arises whether *kairos*, like *aevum*, isn't a rootless fantasy rather than a heuristic fiction. Probably most will agree that one does, without thinking much about it, make some sort of conceptual distinction between two modes of temporality. In other words, we are aware that some occurrences in time are perceived as distinct from *chronos*, from ordinary time. Yet since these occurrences, though lacking the usual qualities of ordinary or passing time, are clearly not eternal, it seems reasonable to think of them as having a different temporal mode, one that can perhaps be investigated by psychologists, or, alternatively, given the description borrowed from the order of time assigned by St. Thomas to angels; or, possibly, dealt with in some quite other way.

However, as I remarked earlier, I do not recall that discussions of the book, which had plenty to say about "tick-tock," for instance, paid any attention to *aevum*, as described in the third chapter above, or proposed other ways of dealing with the subject it was designed to address. I was a little disappointed that the notion escaped serious comment. It is hard to know whether such lacunae in critical comment occur because of a general agreement that the topic is not worth going into, or because it is too baffling, or obviously wrong in ways it might be fruitless to examine. But it would be ungrateful for me to end by expressing disappointment about such matters. It cannot be other than gratifying that the book seems to have continued to interest readers for thirty-odd years, and it would be highly presumptuous in any critic to ask for more attention than that.

NOTES

CHAPTER I

5: In *Homer*. See Georg Róppen and Richard Sommer, *Strangers and Pilgrims*, Oslo, 1964, pp. 19 and 355; Rhys Carpenter, *Folk Tale, Fiction and Saga in the Homeric Epics*, Berkeley, 1958; and Erich Auerbach, *Mimesis*, translated by Willard Trask, Princeton, 1953.

7: *in the middest*. '... a Poet thrusteth into the middest, euen where it most concerneth him, and there recoursing to the thinges forepaste, and diuining of thinges to come, maketh a pleasing analysis of all.' Sir Philip Sidney, *Apology for Poetry*.

D. H. Lawrence and Austin Farrar. See *Apocalypse*, London, 1932, and *The Rebirth of Images*, London, 1949.

Harold Rosenberg. See *The Tradition of the New*, New York, 1962.

Ortega. See Ortega y Gasset, *Man and Crisis*, New York, 1958.

Jaspers. See K. Jaspers, *Man in the Modern Age*, London, 1951, Introduction.

9: *Bultmann*. See R. Bultmann, *The Presence of Eternity*, New York, 1957.

10: *Focillon*. See Henri Focillon, *L'An mil*, Paris, 1952.

13: *a long life*. See, for example, M. W. Bloomfield, 'Penetration of Joachism into Northern Europe,' *Speculum* xxix (1954), 772ff.; R. Freyhan, 'Joachism and the English Apocalypse,' *Journal of the Warburg and Courtauld Institutes*, xviii (1955), 221ff.; Ruth Kestenberg-Gladstein, 'The Third Reich,' in the same issue of the *Warburg Journal;* and the works of Norman Cohn and Eric Hobsbawm mentioned below.

Blake's Everlasting Gospel. See A. L. Morton, *The Everlasting Gospel*, London, 1958.

13: *survive in D. H. Lawrence.* See my 'Spenser and the Allegorists' (British Academy Lecture), London, 1963.

14: *Norman Cohn.* See his *The Pursuit of the Millennium,* London, 1957.

Eric Hobsbawm. See his *Primitive Rebels,* Manchester, 1959.

15: *Fr. Cyril Marystone.* See his *The Coming Type of the End of the World,* Beirut, 1963.

16: *Festinger.* See L. Festinger, *When Prophecy Fails,* New York, 1964.

19: *Robbe-Grillet.* See Alain Robbe-Grillet, *Pour un nouveau roman,* Paris, 1963, p. 168. Other quotations from the recent translation by Barbara Wright in *Snapshots and Towards a New Novel,* London, 1965 (published 1966).

22: *Henry James.* In the Preface to *Roderick Hudson.*

25: *Collingwood.* See R. G. Collingwood, *The Idea of History,* Oxford, 1949.

Butterfield. See Herbert Butterfield, *Christianity and History,* London, 1949.

Bultmann. See Rudolf Bultmann, *History and Eschatology,* New York, 1957.

Winklhofer. As quoted in U. Simon, *The End Is Not Yet,* Welwyn, 1964, p. 57.

26: *Pieper.* See Josef Pieper, *The End of Time,* London, 1954, p. 20. And see also H. H. Rowley, *The Relevance of Apocalyptic,* London, 1946. E. Lampert, *The Apocalypse of History,* London, 1958, p. 54, considers the existentialist position that 'every situation is an "end." '

Popper. See Karl Popper, *The Open Society and Its Enemies,* London, 1945, II, 261.

28: *Focillon.* See Henri Focillon, *The Life of Forms in Art,* translated by C. B. Hogan and George Kubler, revised ed., New York, 1958.

CHAPTER II

36: *Ogden.* See C. K. Ogden, *Bentham's Theory of Fictions,* London, 1932.

    Richards. See I. A. Richards, *The Philosophy of Rhetoric,* New York, 1936.

37: *Ortega.* See his *Man and Crisis,* translated by Mildred Adams, New York, 1958.

38: *Hannah Arendt.* See her *Between Past and Future,* New York, 1963.

40: *Vaihinger.* See Hans Vaihinger, *The Philosophy of As If,* translated by C. K. Ogden, London, 1924.

41: *Vaihinger.* Op. cit., pp. 12-13.

43: *Becker.* See Carl Becker, *The Heavenly City of the Eighteenth Century Philosophers,* New Haven, 1932.

44: *déjà vu,* etc. See G. J. Whitrow, *The Natural Philosophy of Time,* New York, 1959.

45: *Fraisse.* See Paul Fraisse, *The Psychology of Time,* London, 1964.

47: *Cullmann.* See Oscar Cullmann, *Christ and Time,* London, 1951.

    Marsh. See John Marsh, *The Fullness of Time,* New York, 1952.

48: *Helen Gardner.* See her *The Limits of Literary Criticism,* Oxford, 1956.

    James T. Barr. See his *Biblical Words for Time,* London, 1962.

50: *cargo-cults.* See P. M. Worsley, *The Trumpet Shall Sound,* London, 1957, and P. Lawrence, *Road Belong Cargo,* Manchester, 1964.

51: *Poulet.* See Georges Poulet, *Studies in Human Time,* translated by Elliott Coleman, Baltimore, 1956.

52: *Langer.* See Suzanne K. Langer, *Feeling and Form,* London, 1953.

    Curtius. See E. Curtius, *European Literature in the Latin Middle Ages,* translated by W. R. Trask, New York, 1953.

52: *ziggurat.* See Grace E. Cairns, *Philosophies of History*, New York, 1962, and Mircea Eliade, *The Sacred and the Profane*, New York, 1959, p. 40.

53: *Gombrich.* See E. H. Gombrich, 'Moment and Movement in Art,' *Journal of the Warburg and Courtauld Institutes* xxvi (1964), 293ff.

55: *a transformation of the present.* See Fraisse, *The Psychology of Time*, p. 196.

56: *Hannah Arendt.* See *Between Past and Future*, p. 28.

Gentile. See 'The Transcending of Time in History,' in *Philosophy and History*, ed. Klibanski and Paton, Oxford, 1936.

57: *a modern Freudian.* See Norman O. Brown, *Life Against Death*, New York, 1959, p. 95.

a sense of time. Fraisse, *Psychology of Time*, p. 163.

60: *a special case.* See W. Heisenberg, *Physics and Philosophy*, New York, 1962.

61: *Bridgman.* See P. W. Bridgman, *The Way Things Are*, New York, 1959.

Dr. von Franz. See 'Science and the Unconscious,' in Carl G. Jung, *Man and His Symbols*, London, 1964.

63: *George Kubler.* See his *The Shape of Time*, New Haven, 1962.

CHAPTER III

The opening pages of this chapter owe a general debt to Etienne Gilson, *Christian Philosophy in the Middle Ages*, London, 1950, and to Frederick Coplestone, S.J., *A History of Philosophy: II, Mediaeval Philosophy*, London, 1950. Anybody who ventures to write about *aevum* is also indebted not only to the work of Kantorowicz cited below, but to F. H. Brabant's *Time and Eternity in Christian Thought*, 1937. See, too, the article *ævum* in *Dictionnaire de théologie catholique*, vol. 5, Paris, 1939.

71: *Ouspensky and J. B. Priestley.* See the latter's *Man and Time*, London, 1964.

Thomas Mann. See his *Die Entstehung des Doktor Faustus*, Amsterdam, 1949, pp. 192-3, quoted by Margaret Church, *Time and Reality*, Chapel Hill, 1963, pp. 163-4.

73: *Ernst Kantorowicz.* See his *The King's Two Bodies*, Princeton, 1957.

Aristotle. See *De Anima,* 415b13, *Economics,* 134b24, and *De Generatione,* 331a8; also Plato, *Laws,* 721. The passages are discussed in Hannah Arendt, *Between Past and Future,* New York, 1963, pp. 42, 230.

77: *Robert Ellrodt.* See his *Neoplatonism in Spenser,* Paris, 1961.

84: *compared . . . to irony.* By Lock; see S. H. Butcher, *Aristotle's Theory of Poetry and Fine Art,* New York, 1951, p. 331n.

86: *Tilley.* See M. P. Tilley, *A Dictionary of the Proverbs in England,* Ann Arbor, 1950.

87: *'. . . I waited.'* *Paradise Regained,* i. 269.

CHAPTER IV

93: *Auerbach.* See Erich Auerbach, *Mimesis,* translated by Willard Trask, Princeton, 1953, and *Literary Language and Its Public,* translated by Ralph Manheim, London, 1965.

94: *McLuhan.* See H. M. McLuhan, *The Gutenberg Galaxy,* London, 1962, and *Understanding Media,* London, 1964.

Sorokin. See P. A. Sorokin, *Social Philosophies in an Age of Crisis,* London, 1952.

95: *Trilling.* See, for example, *Beyond Culture,* London, 1966.

102: *Rosenberg.* See Harold Rosenberg, *The Tradition of the New,* New York, 1962, and *The Anxious Object,* New York, 1964.

103: *Gombrich.* See E. H. Gombrich, *Art and Illusion,* London, 1960, and *Meditations on a Hobby Horse,* London, 1963.

108: *. . . overt effect.* For a study of this idea see Alfred Stein, 'Fiction and Myth in History,' *Diogenes* 42 (1963), pp. 98ff.

109: *demonic host.* See Norman Cohn, *The Pursuit of the Millennium,* London, 1957, p. 63.

112: *Sartre.* See J.-P. Sartre, *Situations,* translated by Benita Esler, London, 1965, p. 216.

117: *Hassan.* See Ihab Hassan, 'The Subtracting Machine,' *Critique* (1963), 4ff.

118: *Emmett Williams.* See *Times Literary Supplement,* 6 August and 3 September, 1964.

122: *Bailiff . . . Kreisler.* For a relevant and thorough comment see Geoffrey Wagner, *Wyndham Lewis,* London, 1957.

CHAPTER V

129: *Ortega.* See Ortega y Gasset, *Meditations on Don Quixote,* translated by Evelyn Rugg and Diego Martin, New York, 1961, pp. 135ff.

130: *Iris Murdoch.* See 'Against Dryness,' *Encounter,* January 1961.

Mrs. Byatt. See A. S. Byatt, *Degrees of Freedom: The Novels of Iris Murdoch,* London, 1965.

132: *Tillich.* See Paul Tillich, *The Courage To Be,* London, 1952.

134: *autobiography.* See J.-P. Sartre, *Les Mots,* Paris, 1964; *The Words,* translated by Irène Cleophane, London, 1964.

Other works of Sartre referred to in this chapter are *L'Etre et le néant,* Paris, 1943 (translated as *Being and Nothingness* by Hazel E. Barnes, London, 1957); *La Nausée,* Paris, 1938 (translated by Lloyd Alexander, New York, 1959); *Les Chemins de la liberté,* Paris, 1945, 1945, 1949 (translated by Eric Sutton and Gerard Hopkins as *Roads to Freedom—The Age of Reason, The Reprieve, Troubled Sleep,* New York, 1947, 1947, 1950); *Literary Essays,* translated by Annette Michelson, New York, 1955; *Qu'est-ce que la littérature?* (in *Situations II,* Paris, 1948) (translated by Bernard Frechtman, New York, 1949); *L'Existentialisme est un humanisme,* Paris, 1946 (translated as *Existentialism and Humanism* by Philip Mairet, London, 1948).

135: *Mary Warnock.* See Mary Warnock, *The Philosophy of Sartre,* London, 1965, p. 32.

138: *Megaric.* See W. D. Ross, *Aristotle,* New York, 1959, p. 173.

140: *Simone de Beauvoir.* See *La Force de l'âge,* Paris, 1960 (translated as *The Prime of Life* by Peter Green, London, 1965, p. 543).

142: *Kott.* See Jan Kott, *Shakespeare Our Contemporary,* translated by B. Taborski, New York, 1964.

144: *Simone Weil.* See Simone Weil, *La Pesanteur et la grâce*, Paris, 1947; translated as *Gravity and Grace* by Emma Crauford, London, 1952, p. 28.

145: *Philip Thody.* See Philip Thody, *Jean-Paul Sartre*, London, 1960, p. 14.

146: *Melancholia.* See Simone de Beauvoir, *The Prime of Life*, p. 284.

149: *Claude-Edmonde Magny.* See C.-E. Magny, 'The Duplicity of Being,' in *Sartre* (Twentieth Century Views), edited by Edith Kern, Englewood, N.J., 1962, pp. 21ff.

150: *Fredric Jameson.* See his *Sartre: The Origins of a Style*, New Haven, 1961.

151: *Robbe-Grillet.* See Alain Robbe-Grillet, *Pour un nouveau roman*, Paris, 1963, p. 165.

152: *Peter Brooks.* See his 'In the Laboratory of the Novel,' *Dædalus*, Spring 1963, pp. 265ff.

CHAPTER VI

156: *Christopher Burney.* See *Solitary Confinement*, London, 1952, 2nd ed., 1961; Four Square paper, 1964.

167: *Toulmin and Goodfield.* See Stephen Toulmin and June Goodfield, *The Discovery of Time*, London, 1965.

168: *Earl Wasserman.* See Earl R. Wasserman, *The Subtler Language*, Baltimore, 1959.

172: *J. Hillis Miller.* See J. Hillis Miller, *The Disappearance of God*, London, 1963, pp. 17ff.

174: *George Eliot.* See the letters to Sarah Hennell and John Blackwood quoted in Miriam Allott, *Novelists on the Novel*, London, 1959, p. 250.

176: *Joseph Frank.* See 'Spatial Form in Modern Literature,' in *The Widening Gyre*, New Brunswick, N.J., 1963.

177: *Arnold Goldman.* See his *The Joyce Paradox*, London, 1966.

179: *Philip Larkin.* See his 'Reference Back,' in *The Whitsun Weddings*, London, 1964.

NOTES TO EPILOGUE

1 "Revelation," in *The Literacy Guide to the Bible*, ed. Alter and Kermode, Cambridge, Mass., Harvard University Press, 1987, p. 539.
2 For a detailed study see David Ewing Duncan, *The Calendar*, London: Fourth Estate, 1998.
3 Some of these issues are rather entertainingly discussed in *Addressing Frank Kermode: Essays in Criticism and Interpretation*, ed. Margaret Tudeau-Clayton and Martin Warner, London: Macmillan, 1991. I return to the topic below.
4 *Time and Narrative*, Chicago: Chicago University Press, 1984; Wolfgang Iser, *The Fictive and the Imaginary*, Baltimore: The Johns Hopkins University Press, 1993.
5 *Poetry and Prose of William Blake*, ed. Geoffrey Keynes, London: The Nonesuch Press, 1939, p. 637.
6 *I Henry IV*, V. iv. 81–3.
7 See *The Genesis of Secrecy*, Cambridge, Mass.: Harvard University Press, 1979.
8 "Trances," in *The Paperback Tree* (London: Minerva, 1993) reprinted in *Real Voices on Reading*, ed. Philip Davis, London, Macmillan, 1997, p. 77.
9 Iser, *op. cit.* Chapter 4

Printed in the United States
1224100001B/50-68